"For Americans, freedom is an entrenched part of our national identity. But many of us have translated this iconic value into a posture of indulgence. We are free to buy what we want, say what we want and do what we want without regard to others or the environment. Mark and Lisa Scandrette have turned that notion of freedom on its head—we are free to embrace limitation, self-denial and simplicity. The good life as defined by the 'American dream' usually includes a large home, multiple vehicles and fabulous amounts of disposable income. This book is an invitation toward a new vision of the good life, and it provides the tools necessary to take inventory of how we allocate our resources and apply them toward a better, more biblical and more sustainable vision. *Free: Spending Your Time and Money on What Matters Most* is detox for the soul. It leads us out of lives that are mired in material and temporal clutter. It is a gift to all of us who find that there is never enough time and money to live well."

Scott Bessenecker, associate director of missions, InterVarsity Christian Fellowship, and author of *How to Inherit the Earth*

FREE

Spending Your Time and Money
on What Matters Most

Mark Scandrette

with Lisa Scandrette

Foreword by Richard Rohr

IVP Books

An imprint of InterVarsity Press
Downers Grove, Illinois

InterVarsity Press
P.O. Box 1400, Downers Grove, IL 60515-1426
World Wide Web: www.ivpress.com
Email: email@ivpress.com

InterVarsity Press® *is the book-publishing division of InterVarsity Christian Fellowship/USA*®*, a movement of students and faculty active on campus at hundreds of universities, colleges and schools of nursing in the United States of America, and a member movement of the International Fellowship of Evangelical Students. For information about local and regional activities, write Public Relations Dept., InterVarsity Christian Fellowship/USA, 6400 Schroeder Rd., P.O. Box 7895, Madison, WI 53707-7895, or visit the IVCF website at www.intervarsity.org.*

All Scripture quotations, unless otherwise indicated, are taken from the HOLY BIBLE, NEW INTERNATIONAL VERSION®*, NIV*® *Copyright* © *1973, 1978, 1984, 2010 by Biblica, Inc.*™ *Used by permission. All rights reserved worldwide.*

While all stories in this book are true, some names and identifying information in this book have been changed to protect the privacy of the individuals involved.

Cover design: Cindy Kiple
Interior design: Beth Hagenberg
Images: town of music: Ken Jacobsen/Getty Images
          sketched banner: ©*Aleksandar Velasevic/iStockphoto*
ISBN 978-0-8308-3649-9

Printed in the United States of America ∞

Library of Congress Cataloging-in-Publication Data

Scandrette, Mark.
  Free : spending your time and money on what matters most / Mark Scandrette, with Lisa Scandrette.
    pages cm
  Includes bibliographical references.
  ISBN 978-0-8308-3649-9 (pbk. : alk. paper)
  1. Wealth—Religious aspects—Christianity. 2. Values. 3. Christian stewardship. I. Title.
  BR115.W4S23 2013
  241'.68--dc23

                                                                                    2013007722

P	19	18	17	16	15	14	13	12	11	10	9	8	7	6	5	4	3	2	1
Y	29	28	27	26	25	24	23	22	21	20	19	18	17	16	15	14	13

Mark

For my father, Rich, who taught me to be intentional, frugal and generous, and invited me to live into the question "What Matters Most?" And for my mother, Barb, who showed me how to celebrate life, shop resourcefully and love courageously.

Lisa

For my mom, Susan Sands, who modeled contentment and resourcefulness. And for my dad, Jim Sands, who showed me the joy in generosity and trusted God for my future.

Contents

Foreword

M*any before me and the wise* Mark and Lisa Scandrette have said something like "Your checkbook and your calendar reveal your actual belief system." Religious faith that does not become this real and this practical is largely an illusion and a pretense for the human ego and for the world. It really does come down to how we use our time and our money. These reveal the real "gods before us."

Jesus makes the point in the Sermon on the Mount that "where your treasure is, there your heart will be" (Matthew 6:21). And yet I might dare to reverse his statement and say, "Where your heart is, there your treasure will also be." I think that where we offer our heart soon enough determines where we place our financial interest and our daily attention. Both are true. And in either case, they follow one another.

It is interesting to me, actually, that Jesus uses the word *heart* at all. Is this teaching mere sentiment? Lightweight religious feeling? Or was he way ahead of his time in recognizing what neurobiology and groups like HeartMath are only discovering scientifically today? We now know that there are millions of neurons in the heart region, that the heart does "know" things, passionately—for good and for ill. Deep beliefs and convictions are held there, and the mind usually follows to validate the inner passion—even among people who think they are pure intellectuals. So all of our Valentines and romantic songs were not about mere emotion and passing feelings.

This heart center often determines what we do see and what we do not see, what we give credence to and what we deny, what we "irrationally" love and what we "irrationally" fear—but now "rationally" we think. So I can see why often heart-based congregations, with exciting arm-raising worship, warm fellowship and people who pray from their hearts in their own words (we Catholics tend to read prayers!), often bear *much good fruit in the long run.* I have seen it again and again.

This is not to say that head should not be brought to work together with heart. Many evangelical and Pentecostal Christians would help themselves—and the rest of the world tremendously—if they would do a little honest study and reading outside of their rather small comfort zone. So maybe I will add a third thing that reveals your actual belief system: the only way we know that you are in love with God and not just your own self-image is whether you *do* go outside of your own comfort zone!

If you are a white middle-class American, for example, and all your beliefs end up making God look like a white middle-class American, sharing all of your usual prejudices and illusions, I doubt whether you have met the Eternal God at all. You surely have not met Jesus, who always took the side of the outsider, the handicapped, the excluded and the poor. That hardly needs any demonstration since it tends to be the narrative of most of the four Gospels.

Christianity is in such a state of defensiveness and "circling the wagons" today, in great part because we have not taken the time to make the gospel something beyond an exclusionary ideology that merely serves our needs. People do not trust or admire us anymore as a result.

People are not sure of what or who we Christians love, but they sure know who we do not love, and from our historical record they also know that we do love war, arms, possessions, pleasure, control and social honor—things far removed from one of Jesus' strongest and clearest dichotomies, "You cannot serve both God and *the system*" (my translation of Luke 16:13 and Matthew 6:24, and a fair one I think). Amazing that we made such *absolutes* of other things that

Jesus never talked about at all, while here he is *absolutely* definitive and we explain it away.

I sincerely thank Mark and Lisa for taking the time to write something very concrete, practical and programmatic for us, while being very inspiring and hopeful at the same time. This book is "definitive." By that I mean it is clear and helpful—and in a very kind way. This is not more ideology from above, not guilt from below. I am honored to write a few words to encourage your reading here, and just hope my own kind of definitiveness is not the kiss of death to something that could truly open your mind, your heart, and your entire worldview to God's big picture.

Fr. Richard Rohr, O.F.M.
Center for Action and Contemplation
Albuquerque, New Mexico

Why We Wrote This Book

We *live in one of the wealthiest economies* on earth. Yet many of us feel crunched for time, stressed in our finances or perplexed about what makes life meaningful. Our culture is driven by a sense of scarcity, fear and an unquenchable quest for more. If we don't make conscious choices to resist these impulses, the force of a materialistic and consumeristic society will make most of our decisions for us. The scripts we've inherited about material prosperity are wearing us out, robbing our joy and destroying the planet.

A CRISIS OF MONEY, MEANING AND GLOBAL SUSTAINABILITY

If you are reading this book, you are very likely in the top 5-10 percent of global wealth. As people living in postindustrialized countries we must wrestle with our contribution to the crisis of global inequity and ecological destruction. The 12 percent of us who live in Western Europe and North America are responsible for 60 percent of global private consumption.[1] We should be haunted by estimates that it

---

[1]"State of the World 2004: Richer, Fatter, and Not Much Happier," Worldwatch Institute, accessed December 4, 2012, www.worldwatch.org/node/1785.

would take four to seven earths to sustain us if everyone on the planet had the same ecological footprint as the average American.[2]

Our overconsumption is largely fueled by a debt-based public and private economy. The current US national debt is estimated at $16 trillion.[3] As of September 2012 the average American household was $6,772 in debt, with the average indebted household owing $15,328 to creditors.[4] If we feel strapped in one of the wealthiest and most stable economies in the world, what about the nearly three billion people on earth who are living on less than $2 a day?[5]

Our challenge is to pursue a standard of living that can be shared by all. To love our neighbor as ourselves we have to consider how our individual actions affect our sister across the street and our brother on another continent. We might not be able to fully grasp the scope of the problem or offer a complete solution, but we can wrestle with the weight of our relative privilege and disproportionate consumption. For the sake of our global neighbors, the planet and future generations we've got to find a way to be less wasteful and consumptive, discovering a more sustainable version of the American Dream.

We are encouraged by the growing awareness among people of faith that the gospel of Jesus is holistic and touches every aspect of our lives. We see Christians of every variety desiring a life of faith that includes being a good neighbor, valuing relationships, cultivating an inner life, caring about people affected by poverty and consciously becoming better stewards of creation. However, this good vision for the church will remain largely unrealized unless practical realities and competencies are addressed. Many of us are

---

[2]Robynne Boyd, "One Footprint at a Time," *Scientific American,* July 14, 2011, http://blogs.scientificamerican.com/plugged-in/2011/07/14/one-footprint-at-a-time.

[3]U.S. National Debt Clock, accessed December 4, 2012, www.brillig.com/debt_clock.

[4]"American Household Credit Card Debt Statistics Through 2012," *NerdWallet.com,* accessed December 4, 2012, www.nerdwallet.com/blog/credit-card-data/average-credit-card-debt-household.

[5]"The State of Consumption Today," Worldwatch Institute, accessed December 4, 2012, www.worldwatch.org/node/810.

too busy or distracted to sustain a life of compassionate engagement. We live lives of hurry, worry and striving, finding little satisfaction in our manic work and recreational activities. Instead of being free to create beauty, nurture relationships and seek the greater good, many of us feel stuck in lives dictated by the need to pay bills or maintain a certain (often consumptive) standard of living. We can't have it all—the prevailing level of consumption, a life of deeper meaning and relationships and global equity and sustainability. To realize these good dreams we must adjust our values and practices and seek creative solutions.

Few things in life shape us more than our choices about how we earn, spend, save and invest. Most of us will spend a third of our time at income-producing jobs. How we choose to manage those earnings largely determines whether we are free to serve the greater good. Yet, rarely have religious communities, in particular, done well at addressing money and work as areas for discipleship—other than the occasional sermon about giving. Perhaps we unconsciously tend to separate money and work from the center of our religious lives, making an artificial and unhelpful distinction between what is spiritual and what is temporal, and thereby less important. In a holistic understanding of the gospel every part of life is sacred and integral to what it means to be a follower of Jesus. This means we must learn to talk more honestly and openly about the details of our financial lives as an essential aspect of Christian discipleship.

The current generation coming of age is hopeful and motivated to seek solutions to the world's greatest problems. Students today are passionate about issues of global justice, including poverty and human trafficking, and want to make a difference. Often these dreams are in conflict with family expectations: "We didn't spend $150,000 on your education so that you could waste your life as a non-profit worker living in a slum." Often the impediments are more personal and practical. Students today make financial decisions between the ages of eighteen and twenty-four that will largely shape how they will spend the next thirty to forty years of their lives. Many will leave school with significant debt. Some will go on to graduate school, incurring further debt. Most will unconsciously adopt the culture's habits of consumption. We've sadly watched many young people who had amazing and creative ambitions settle into dream-killing debt-maintenance jobs. We believe that with strategic action this pattern can be changed.

This book addresses the unique challenges and opportunities presented to people living within the dominant culture of the postindustrial world, a culture that places particular value on material prosperity, instant gratification, debt-based economic growth and rapid economic progress. We recognize that people living with less privilege under other circumstances might have different primary issues to address—though we believe that a perspective of abundance and the practices of gratitude, trust, contentment and generosity translate across cultures.

We hope to offer a resource that connects personal economic practice with spiritual values, questions of meaning, global justice and ecological sustainability. To do this we'll touch on topics like taxes, insurance and debt reduction, but this book is not intended to be authoritative in matters of tax law, banking or investing. For specific guidance on these and other matters we recommend seeking specialized resources or consulting with a qualified tax accountant or trusted financial adviser.

It's often easier to talk about the national debt than our personal finances, or to complain about predatory lending and the evil of corporations than to face the greed that resides within. While the impact of larger systems should not be minimized, our primary focus here is on personal values, beliefs and financial practices. If we believe "another world is possible," then the place to begin is with ourselves—choosing to surrender our personal kingdoms to the good dreams of God for our world.

CORE BELIEFS

The gospel invites us into a life of radical contentment, generosity, gratitude, trust and simplicity. We can reimagine our assumptions about time, money and material possessions to pursue a life of greater freedom, leveraging our time and resources toward what matters most.

Three core beliefs have shaped the development of this book:

1. We were created with a purpose, to seek the greater good of God's loving reign. Human beings long for a deeper sense of purpose. According to Jesus, we "are the light of the world" (Matthew 5:14), created to do and bring good to this world (Ephesians 2:10). The wisdom of this teaching encourages us to stretch beyond the mundane concerns of our lives to be animated by a calling to be agents of healing and restoration.

2. We have enough. The ancient voices of Scripture affirm that we live in a world of abundance, where the Creator provides all that we need. "You [God] . . . satisfy the desires of every living thing"(Psalm 145:16). Rain falls and sun shines on the earth, producing the goods that sustain us. We are invited to celebrate this abundance with thanks, to trust God for what we need, to be content with what we have and to share with those who are hungry, thirsty, naked, sick and lonely.

3. We can make intentional choices about how we spend our time and money. We've been given incredible power to imagine, learn, grow and choose how we want to live. Living well requires vision, self-awareness, discipline and the development of practical skills. As those created just "a little lower than angels and crowned . . . with glory and honor" (Psalm 8:5), we can make choices to become more content and free to spend our time and resources on what matters most. We think that to make life-giving changes that last, we need a source of energy and love greater than our own. The promise of the gospel of life is that if we do what we can, God will

help us do what we cannot under our own strength (Philippians 2:12-13).

This book is the result of our lifelong journey exploring and integrating these core beliefs into our lives. While for the sake of clarity this book was written in Mark's voice, it is our shared story. Lisa's voice will appear at the beginning of chapter three and in many of the sidebars (along with occasional observations by our daughter Hailey). Simplicity is one of the vows of the intentional community we helped form and participate in. Seven years ago we began leading workshops on simple living and invited participants into practice-based groups where they were supported as they took steps to simplify their lives. Over the years we developed and refined the six-week curriculum used in those groups, which is the basis for the tasks and exercises contained in these pages. This book is a follow-up and specific application of Mark's previous book, *Practicing the Way of Jesus,* in which he advocates for an action- and group-based approach to spiritual formation.

We can choose to pursue meaning, value people, engage the world's needs and move toward a rate of consumption that is more globally sustainable and equitable. We can be free to spend our time and money on what matters most.

How to Use This Book

❀

We imagine you are reading this book because, like us, you're searching for a way to live more gratefully, creatively and sustainably. That journey takes great courage, and we hope this book can offer some help along the way. Your story and the good dreams that are deep inside of you are important and unique. We believe that the steps in this book can move you toward a life of greater financial freedom, deeper meaning and a lifestyle that is more sustainable—personally and globally.

Our goal is to help you develop a perspective and practices that empower you to be as free and fruitful as you can be, living from a deep sense of purpose for the greater good. We've designed this book with seven steps to help you clarify your life vision and values; cultivate practices of gratitude, trust, contentment and generosity; and develop practical skills to align your money and time with the deeper goals and values you've identified.

The seven steps are

1. Name what matters most to you.

2. Value and align your time.

3. Practice gratitude and trust.

4. Believe you have enough.

5. Create a spending plan.

6. Maximize your resources.

7. Live generously and spend wisely.

Through each of these steps we are inviting you to live into the question, How can I be free to pursue what matters most—to risk being fully alive? In order to help you accomplish these steps, each chapter includes tasks, exercises, experiments and conversation questions.

Exercises are designed to be done while you are reading the chapter. These will help you to prepare your heart and mind to complete the tasks. Most chapters include self-evaluation surveys designed to help you reflect on where you are and where you want to be. Journal entry prompts are also included to encourage you to explore your story and reflect on what has shaped your perspective and practices. We are going to ask you to take an honest look at what your values are, where you spend your time and how you manage your money. That kind of honest assessment and transparency may seem scary. But trust us, taking an unflinching look at how you've been adversely affected by certain choices is one step toward a better way. We all have unhealthy patterns with time, money and consumption, which have led to things like worry, busyness, debts, obesity, clutter, stinginess or obsessive frugality. We're invited to face these struggles with honesty, believing that we were made for something better. Facing these shadows brings them into the light where they no longer have power over us. If we first deal with heart issues (our beliefs, attitudes, motives and way of seeing), the practical details of how we manage our money, time and possessions are navigated more easily.

Experiments are actions we will be inviting you to take to help you become more self-aware and to integrate what you learn into your everyday life. We start from where we are to move toward greater wholeness. If you feel discouraged or trapped by your current situation, we invite you to discern your next step toward abundance, gratefulness, contentment, generosity, sustainability and trust. This book follows an action-reflection method. The experiments are designed to help you become more conscious of your thoughts, motives and behavior, and to risk an action that might open you up to new possibilities. A variety of experiments are included. Choose one that is appropriate to your situation and desire for growth, something that both fits your comfort level and stretches you in some way. If the suggested experiments don't quite fit, feel free to improvise. The key is to do something tangible and measurable to see what effect that action has in your life. Be specific and know that intensity is important.[1]

Tasks are specific assignments to help you develop a tangible plan for spending your time and money. Since this book is something of a time, money and life management boot camp, in each chapter you will be invited to take an intentional step toward more order and clarity in your life. Each task will take between two and six hours. If you complete all the tasks, you will have a comprehensive simplicity plan that you can refer back to, to help you stay on track.[2]

Conversation questions are designed to encourage your further development in dialogue with significant people in your life. It's a lot easier to make changes in life when you take steps along with someone else. We highly recommend working through this book with at least one other person—your spouse, a supportive friend or a small group. If nothing else it would be good to enlist the support of friend who can listen to and encourage you in the process. A friend or group of friends can give you the positive peer pressure and support to make changes that would be more difficult on your own. In each chapter you will find questions to spark conversation. (If you plan to go

---

[1]For a more detailed explanation of the dynamics of spiritual formation and group experimentation, see Mark's book *Practicing the Way of Jesus* (Downers Grove, IL: InterVarsity Press, 2011).

[2]A digital copy of this plan is available online for download at www.ivpress.com.

through this book with a friend or group of friends, a group study guide is included as well as access to eight online video curriculum sessions.)

The exercises in this book can be done in eight weeks, but it might be worth spending extended time working through the steps and chapters over twelve to sixteen weeks if time allows.

A Prayer of Abundance

In the process of growth and change, you may find it helpful to have a daily meditation to guide your thoughts, remind you of your intentions and call on God's help. Consider using the following prayer each day as you work through the steps in this book.

I know that I am cared for by an abundant Provider.
I choose to be grateful and trusting.
I believe I have enough and that what I need
will always be provided.
I choose to be content and generous.
I know that my choices matter for myself, for others
and for future generations.
Help me to live consciously and creatively, celebrating signs
of your new creation that is present and coming.
Creator, who made me to seek the greater good of your kingdom,
Guide me to use my time, talents and resources
to pursue what matters most.
Teach me to be free,
to live without worry, fear or greed in the freedom of your abundance.

Give me my daily bread, as I share with those in need.

Thank you for the precious gift of life!

Which line of the prayer do you most resonate with?

Are there any statements in the prayer that you struggle to believe or sound too good to be true? Why?

Introduction

Making Space for Life to Grow

The seed that fell among thorns stands for those who hear,
but as they go on their way they are choked by
life's worries, riches and pleasures,
and they do not mature.
But the seed on good soil stands for those with a noble
and good heart, who hear the word, retain it,
and by persevering produce a crop.

LUKE 8:14-15

G*rowing up, my family was a bit odd.* In the 1970s, when most people who could moved to the suburbs, we bought a little house in an older part of the city.[1] In an era of dual incomes, conspicuous

---

[1]We are not suggesting that an urban life is preferable to a rural or suburban life, or that a life of simplicity is more achievable in an urban setting. Each context—urban, suburban or

consumption and shopping malls, my family chose to live on one salary, my dad's Army Reserve job, and my mom made the unfashionable choice to stay home to raise us four kids. I was the kid with the brown bag lunches and high-water, hand-me-down jeans. We owned one car, a rusty old station wagon with fake wood paneling that sat in our garage most of the week. Rain or shine my dad biked five miles to work each way in his military fatigues. For much of my childhood, our television was under lock and key. Six of us shared one bathroom, which made getting ready for school and church a challenge—creatively solved by having one person on the toilet and another in the shower, with a third person at the sink brushing their teeth.

Being odd in the ways we were had some advantages. We knew our neighbors well and went to local schools and shops. Mom had time to make nutritious meals and to be a hospitable neighbor and caring friend. Dad's job allowed him to be home by 4:30 each day. After dinner we had many leisurely hours to enjoy reading and discussing books at the table, playing volleyball in the backyard or going on walks together along the Mississippi river. Our life was simple, connected and largely local.

When I was twelve Dad accepted a promotion that would provide new opportunities and pay $10,000 more a year—a lot of money back then. But the job required him to transfer to a new city every three or four years. The summer before my senior year we moved from Minneapolis to rural Alabama. With the money made from selling our small city home, my parents bought a large brick house in the country with a built-in swimming pool on two acres of land. It had four bedrooms, two living rooms, a formal dining room and not one, not two, but four bathrooms! With my dad's larger salary we could afford many things we'd previously gone without: better clothes, a house full of new furniture, stereo equipment and our first home computer. Living

---

rural—offers advantages and challenges to seeking a life of simplicity.

in the country, we quickly became a three-car family. Suddenly we went from being oddly simple to "those rich Yankees out on King's Hollow Road."

Our larger house and pool were great for entertaining, and living in another culture broadened and enriched our horizons, but there were also unanticipated consequences to our new life. Uprooting from where we'd lived for thirteen years was traumatic and often lonely. It took thirty minutes to drive to school, to work or to church activities. With more stuff came more responsibility—cleaning the pool, mowing an acre of lawn, maintaining three vehicles and scrubbing those four bathrooms! Dad traveled regularly, worked late and often came home stressed or exhausted. On good days we celebrated our new opportunities and friendships. On bad days, Dad voiced his doubts about whether the increase in status and pay were worth what we'd lost by moving. His honest reflections about this transition left a lasting impression on me about the trade-offs we make with any decision.

WHAT MATTERS MOST?

When I was in college, beginning to clarify my life vision and values, I compared the two versions of "the good life" that I'd experienced. Of course there were benefits and costs to both circumstances, but I decided that if at some point I had to choose one over the other, meaningful work and relationships were more precious to me than money or things. I felt a hunger awakening inside of me for a life of greater freedom to pursue what matters most.

One of the things that mattered most to me was a girl I'd left behind in Minnesota. Lisa and I met at camp when we were fifteen and sixteen. After moving to Alabama I spent much of my spare time writing letters to Lisa and a lot of my money calling her long distance. During our second year in college, we began to consider marriage. We had an instant connection and over time discovered that we wanted many of the same things out of life: to be God-oriented, to create a loving family, to serve needs and to live simply and creatively. Looking around us, it didn't seem like most people were free to pursue their deeper values and purpose. We began to ask ourselves, "What choices can we make now to be free to pursue what matters most to us in the future?"

Over the next few months Lisa and I talked extensively about our shared dreams. We imagined living in an old house in a large city, raising kids, offering hospitality and caring for needs in our neighborhood. We hoped that one of us would be able to stay at home to nurture our kids, that our home would be a place of hospitality, and that we would be free to spend our time doing work we were passionate about, having the flexibility to work and serve together. We began to realize that our dream was not about a particular job or a career, but more a way of life—and a pretty idealistic one at that. But we also believed that this was the kind of life we were called to, and we would make any sacrifices that were necessary.

What quickly became clear to us was that we wouldn't be able to pursue this dream and an American lifestyle of consumption at the same time. We decided to choose time and freedom over money and stuff. During this process, we began to pay more careful attention to the wise and crazy things that Jesus said about wealth, meaning and material possessions.

Sell your possessions and give to the poor. (Luke 12:33)

Life does not consist in an abundance of possessions. (Luke 12:15)

Do not worry about your life, what you will eat or drink. . . . Seek first [God's] kingdom. (Matthew 6:25, 33)

We began to ask ourselves, "What if we tried to live by these teachings instead of the culturally dominant messages about success, security and prosperity?"

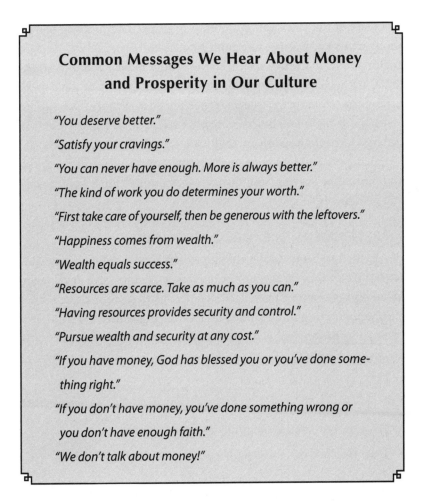

Common Messages We Hear About Money and Prosperity in Our Culture

"You deserve better."

"Satisfy your cravings."

"You can never have enough. More is always better."

"The kind of work you do determines your worth."

"First take care of yourself, then be generous with the leftovers."

"Happiness comes from wealth."

"Wealth equals success."

"Resources are scarce. Take as much as you can."

"Having resources provides security and control."

"Pursue wealth and security at any cost."

"If you have money, God has blessed you or you've done something right."

"If you don't have money, you've done something wrong or you don't have enough faith."

"We don't talk about money!"

We realized that unless we became more conscious and intentional about our financial and vocational choices, the force of a fearful and consumptive culture would make most of our decisions for us. We were already feeling the pressure to follow this script: "Go to college. Study hard. Land a good job. Buy the American Dream." There seemed to be an unspoken expectation that each generation should be more economically and professionally successful than the previous one.

Raised in the Christian faith, both of us grew up hearing stories about saints and heroes, like Saint Francis and Sister Clare, Hudson Taylor and Amy Carmichael, who took more radical and unconventional paths. They quit school, aborted their careers or gave away their possessions to pursue a deeper purpose. What if we started making our decisions based more on a sense of calling than on the material expectations of our culture? Could we find a way to be more content and less consumer oriented, spend less time earning and more time serving, and discover ways to live more consciously and generously?

AN EXPERIMENT IN RADICAL SIMPLICITY

We decided to begin taking risks to experiment with voluntary simplicity. We got engaged, quit our university studies, gave away many of our possessions and moved to the inner city to serve at-risk children and families. The guiding principles for our "experiment" were largely inspired by the ancient Scriptures and the teachings of Jesus:

→ Be grateful and content with what we have.

→ Make work and financial decisions, whenever possible, based on a deeper sense of purpose and calling.

→ Be resourceful and ecologically conscious.

→ Trust God and ask for what we need.

→ Budget and make clear financial plans.

→ Avoid debt.

→ Be generous and use resources (time, money, talents and possessions) to do good.

Before we began, I remember sitting in the library at my university racking my brain to figure out how we could avoid the trap of increased consumption. As a thought experiment I posed the question, What is the minimum amount that a person needs to live? I recalled a comment the apostle Paul made, "If we have food and clothing, we will be content with that" (1 Timothy 6:8). Anticipating a move back to snowy Minneapolis, I decided that in addition to food and clothes, shelter might also be a necessity. I estimated that I would need $300 a month to pay for essentials like housing and groceries. Assuming that I might only make minimum wage, which was $3.80 at the time, I calculated that I would only have to work three or four hours a day. With two people working part-time minimum wage jobs, we could just double the amount needed to $600. Obviously, my calculations didn't account for things like transportation costs or health insurance, but I designated these as nonessential luxuries we could have if we wanted to work more. My calculations convinced me that if we adopted a minimal standard of living, much of our time could be free to pursue other meaningful activities besides paid work.

After we got engaged, I spent the summer traveling across Minnesota, leading weekly kids' clubs in low-income neighborhoods. Since I was staying with people and food was provided, I could do this without pay. In autumn we both got full-time jobs working at a community center in inner-city Minneapolis that served at-risk families and people living on the street. We set our budget based on the minimum amount we needed to live ($600 a month), and since we were both working full time, we saved $8,000 over the next four months. Then another organization invited us to develop a project working with children and families in northern Minnesota, where the iron ore mines had just shut down, resulting in high rates of unemployment, domestic violence and child abuse. We would get to work together and create new programs. The pay was low ($833 a month), which was fine with us because we already knew we could live on less. Over the next four years we had the time of our lives engaging at-risk kids and families, building community and developing our skills. We also took evening courses and completed our college degrees.

Adopting a posture of radical contentment had many benefits. We came to appreciate the small things. Not owning a TV or having money to go to the movies pushed us to seek fun more creativity. We made music, went for walks, read books aloud to one another or invited friends over to cook meals together. Being content almost effortlessly moved us toward a more ecologically and globally sustainable lifestyle—less driving, few nonessential purchases, lowering our thermostat in winter and so on. It's safe to say that spending less gets you at least halfway toward a smaller ecological footprint. By adopting radical contentment we often had money left over each month and at the end of the year—sometimes up to half our modest income. Instead of spending the extra money on ourselves, it made more sense to give the extra we had to someone who needed it more than we did. We were free to give away up to 20 percent of our income and save for upcoming expenses and long-term dreams.

LIVING SIMPLY AS A FAMILY

It was easy to imagine this freedom as a single person and even as a couple, but what about with children? Three years after we were married, our daughter was born, and we decided it might be more economical to own a home instead of renting. We found a small house that we were able to pay for with $11,000 in cash, money we'd saved that even included $2,000 Lisa had earned babysitting when she was a teenager. More like a trailer than a house, it wasn't our dream home, but it was ours—matching the criteria we'd set up when we met with the realtor: two bedrooms and a garage, within seven miles of our work and not a fixer-upper. Even though our income was low, we only spent half of what we made each month, saving the rest for upcoming expenses such as car insurance and the labor and delivery costs for our children (birthing and delivery weren't covered by our policy). We began paying ourselves rent to save up for a down payment, since our long-term vision was to live in a larger cosmopolitan city.

The kids and families we worked with in northern Minnesota thought we were rich because we had a well-kept home, served them good food and went on yearly vacations. In reality we lived on much less than most of their families did. What this showed us was that we had privilege that went beyond material assets. We had advantages because of our education and ethnicity, but even more, we were privileged because our families gave us the skills and insight to use money wisely, teaching us how to budget, save for upcoming expenses, avoid unnecessary debt and shop resourcefully. None of our parents had college degrees when we were growing up. Ours were old-school, do-it-yourself families who faithfully gave away 10 percent or more of their incomes and modeled generosity, love and hospitality in countless ways.

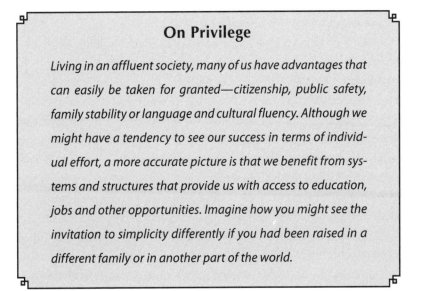

On Privilege

Living in an affluent society, many of us have advantages that can easily be taken for granted—citizenship, public safety, family stability or language and cultural fluency. Although we might have a tendency to see our success in terms of individual effort, a more accurate picture is that we benefit from systems and structures that provide us with access to education, jobs and other opportunities. Imagine how you might see the invitation to simplicity differently if you had been raised in a different family or in another part of the world.

Over the next three years we had two more children, and I became the family pastor at a local church and went to seminary (also paid for in cash). When our kids were one, two and three, we moved to San Francisco to start a neighborhood-based faith community. This was a huge leap for us financially. We anticipated spending more on monthly rent than we'd ever made in monthly salary. To make matters worse, we happened to move during the late 1990s technology boom when there was a less than 1 percent vacancy rate on housing in the city. After looking despairingly through the local real estate listings, I told Lisa that if we wanted to raise our kids in San Francisco, we should expect to spend the next twenty years living in a tiny two-bedroom apartment. Lisa, who had always been better at trusting God than I was, said, "Well, if we are supposed to be here, I'm going to pray that God gives us a home to own that we can afford." I said, "Go ahead and pray, but be prepared to live in a tiny apartment." Lisa's prayer was answered. Through a series of serendipitous circumstances and with the $30,000 down payment we'd saved, we were able to buy a two-unit Victorian building. By renting out the second flat for a modest amount to friends, we were able to pay off the mortgage in just fourteen years.

With the skills and habits we've learned together, along with a bit of luck and a lot of grace, we've largely been free to choose meaningful work and to be generous with our time, talents, money and other resources. We've served together in nonprofit enterprises, educated our three children at home and developed community in an at-risk neighborhood. We've also been able to take on more risky and creative activities that don't necessarily pay well but are deeply satisfying—like mentoring younger people, caring for neighbors and traveling, teaching and writing about integrative spiritual practices. Over the years we've been able to live comfortably on one modest income, often below the poverty line, and have never made more than an average teacher's salary.

The freedom to invest in relationships and pursue the things that matter most to us is more valuable to us than having a larger home, more discretionary income or the promise of an extravagant lifestyle in old age. Life has felt rich and full of feasting, celebration and interesting friends. What makes our journey impressive to some is that we didn't start with an inheritance or other economic advantages, and we've pursued our dreams in San Francisco, one of the most expensive cities in America.

The Cost of Simplicity
Lisa Scandrette

I fully embrace the life we've chosen, but it has not been without challenges. Getting on the same page regarding our budget required hard work. Prior to getting married I spent money on things like gifts, books and long distance phone calls to loved ones. Our shared budget didn't have as much room for these things, and the values of being generous and keeping in touch with my family came into tension with our need to stay within our spending plan. It took time, understanding and persistent communication to create a spending plan that reflected and encompassed all of our values.

The simple way we had chosen sometimes made socializing awkward. Our friends would invite us out to dinner or the movies, which seldom fit in our budget. This left us with three uncomfortable options: explain our finances and decline the invitation, spend money on something we had decided not to spend it on, or let our friends treat us to the meal, which left us feeling like we were "takers" in the relationship if this happened too often. Because we valued our friends, we would often suggest eating at our place or recommend a restaurant that better fit our spending plan.

I love to be able to give generously to others. However, there have been times that I've needed to limit how much I give to stay within a budget. I've learned new ways to give, and that a small gift is often appreciated as much as a lavish one. I tend to give gifts that cost more time than money now, which also end up feeling more meaningful. On this journey I've realized that all choices, though, have a cost. It is a matter of choosing which benefits and costs best fit our values.

A WHISPER OF INVITATION

Over the years we've discovered that our story is not unique. While the specific details may be different, we know many people who have taken intentional and creative steps to become more free to spend their time and money on what matters most to them. We're grateful to have heard the whisper of insight about time, money and freedom early in life—though the invitation comes to each of us at just the right time and is never too late. It came to Jose and Rebecca just after they turned thirty when they decided that it was time to pay off their credit cards and change their spending habits. It came to Ron and Cathy in their midfifties, when they realized they have enough and don't need to find their significance through what they own or achieve. It came to Mike after he retired, when deeper questions of purpose began to resurface after lying dormant following years dedicated to earning and providing. In each of the chapters that follow we'll share a story about someone who has taken steps to be free.

THE FREEDOM OF SIMPLICITY

Most of the world's religious traditions advocate for a path of simplicity, recognizing a tradeoff between material preoccupation and spiritual enlightenment. Earnest seekers since ancient times have committed themselves to lives of voluntary poverty and service, knowing how easily wealth, pleasure and security can become intoxicating and destructive substitutes for the free and open lives we were created for. The parables of the Christian gospel invite us into a life of abundance and vitality, where, like well-watered plants, our lives produce good. You were made for a life of flourishing. We are cared for. We have what we need and can use what we've been given to be fruitful and life giving.

Jesus warned that "life's worries, riches and pleasures" can choke a plant, making it unfruitful (Luke 8:14). What crowds our lives and keeps us from flourishing? Where is true life being choked out by anxiety and stress, striving for success or seeking happiness where it can't be found? It's the voice that says "never enough" or what Father Thomas Keating has called our misplaced "emotional programs for happiness."[2] Though we were created for a life of abundant goodness, we often make choices that limit our freedom to pursue what matters most. Simplicity is about making space in our lives from which good can freely grow.

Simplicity suggests that which is uncomplicated and natural. Sometimes when people hear the word *simplicity* they picture austerity, Spartan home decorating or a green, low-impact lifestyle. While these may all be manifestations of simplicity, we are using the term to describe an overall approach to life. Our favorite definition of simplicity is "choosing to leverage time, money, talents and possessions toward what matters most." It's what Jesus was getting at when he said, "Seek first his kingdom" (Matthew 6:33). In other words, live from a deeper sense of purpose and align your whole life around that purpose. In the language of spiritual formation it is the pursuit of an undivided life, where the mind, the heart and the body move together into the abundance and wholeness we were created for. Life works best when we learn to use our time, talents and possessions in service to the greater good that our Creator desires.

STARTING FROM WHERE YOU ARE

We've often found that the topic of simplicity elicits some strong reactions. "Are you trying to make me feel guilty?" "Are you going to tell me I have to sell my car, cut up my credit cards or stop eating meat?" It's easy to become embarrassed or defensive about what we have (or don't have) or beat ourselves up about the mistakes we've made, but that doesn't really help us change. Shame is not a particularly effective or healthy motivator.

---

[2]See Thomas Keating, *Invitation to Love* (New York: Continuum, 1994).

Simplicity is not a list of rules. Our goal isn't to pressure you to get out of debt, change your job, sell your car or compost your food scraps (though those might be helpful things to do). We don't plan on giving you a list of rules you have to follow or make declarations about what simple people do or do not do. Our goal is to provide resources and opportunities to empower you to take steps to become more free to seek the greater good.

Simplicity is an invitation. A better way of seeing the potential for change is that we are being invited into a more free and fulfilling life that is better than the lives we currently have. That's why having a positive and compelling vision is so important. We've been holding on to things that are crowding and complicating our lives and keeping us from what is really valuable and rewarding. God's invitation to us is always toward life, greater freedom and love.

Simplicity is about your process, not comparisons. Because we are unique individuals, no two people who seek the freedom of simplicity make the exact same choices or have the same challenges. The path to simplicity will look different for each of us, and it will look different at various stages of life. True simplicity begins with the heart and flows into loving action. To pursue simplicity, we attend not only to matters of the inner life—worry, fear, greed, contentment—but also to very practical financial competencies, like budgeting, time management and financial planning.

We don't all have the same growth edges. One person's challenge might be learning to be content and limit consumption while another, who is naturally drawn to austerity, may want to loosen up to enjoy life more. One person may feel challenged to make choices out of their deeper values, while another person may want to learn to take care of practical details like paying bills. Although our growth edges may be different, it's safe to say that anyone seeking simplicity will take steps to (1) address soul issues like gratitude, trust and contentment; (2) develop time and money management skills; (3) explore questions of meaning, vision and values; and (4) choose a lifestyle that is more globally equitable and sustainable.

Simplicity is about progress, not perfection. No one achieves "simplicity perfection," as if such a thing existed. Just take the steps you feel invited into. We invite you to take a playful approach to this book; do the exercises and tasks that seem relevant to you and skip those that don't. Even if you don't finish the steps, don't beat yourself up. It doesn't matter how far you get in the process; you can always pick it up later when you are ready. You should feel good about any steps you take. With that said, you may also want to pay attention to the exercises and tasks you feel the most resistance to. If you find yourself thinking, *I'm definitely not going to cancel my cable sports package!* or *There's no way I'll ever be able to give away 10 percent of my income*—those points of resistance may hold clues about your disordered attachments. A new step in that area may have the most dramatic results.

You were created for a life of flourishing, to experience the fruitfulness that brings good to our world. With a clear vision, a contented soul, and a bit of creative ingenuity and problem solving, each of us can experience the freedom of simplicity. We can take steps to leverage our time and money toward what matters most, making space for life to grow.

> As you anticipate working through the steps in this book, what are you excited about? Where do you feel resistance?
>
> How do you want to be more free?

JOURNAL EXERCISE: WHAT'S YOUR MONEY STORY?

We each have a story and inherited beliefs about money that influence how we make decisions in our lives. As you begin the journey toward greater simplicity, it may be helpful to reflect on the messages and experiences that have shaped your relationship with money. Write a one- to two-page story that explores the major theme(s) or a particular episode that has shaped how you view and use money. You can use the following prompts to get the creative juices flowing. Share your story with a supportive friend or group of friends.

→ In my family, money was a source of . . .

→ I got the impression that we were . . .

→ For my dad money was . . . For my mom money was . . .

→ Something I learned from my parents about money that I now appreciate is . . .

→ One thing I wished I'd learned about money earlier in life is . . .

→ The messages I received about money, success and happiness from my culture were . . .

→ A sense of abundance challenges or subverts the messages I received about money by . . .

→ I believe that money . . .

→ I would like to teach my children, grandchildren or younger people in my life that money and provision . . .

TASK: TIME, MONEY AND MEANING SELF-ASSESSMENT

When it comes to time, money and meaning, each of us have strengths and potential growth areas. As you prepare to take new steps, it will be helpful to value your strengths and identify one or two areas that you would particularly like to grow in. Read the following statements and circle the number that best describes your current situation. Please use the following scheme:

1 = strongly disagree

2 = disagree

3 = undecided

4 = agree

5 = strongly agree

WORK AND MEANING

1. I feel confident about my purpose in life.   1 2 3 4 5
2. I can articulate my vision and values.   1 2 3 4 5
3. I have short-term goals connected to my vision and values.   1 2 3 4 5
4. I spend my time and energy doing what I believe is important.   1 2 3 4 5
5. I see how my work contributes to the greater good.   1 2 3 4 5
6. My work makes me feel vital and energized.   1 2 3 4 5
7. I know what my talents and passions are.   1 2 3 4 5
8. I am using my talents and passions for the good of the world.   1 2 3 4 5
9. I give time and energy to causes and concerns I am passionate about.   1 2 3 4 5
10. I talk about my life goals and deeper values with those closest to me.   1 2 3 4 5

Total: _____

TIME MANAGEMENT

1. I feel good about how I manage my time.   1 2 3 4 5
2. I am rarely rushed or in a hurry.   1 2 3 4 5
3. I plan ahead and make the most important tasks my priorities.   1 2 3 4 5
4. I have a pace of life that is sustainable.   1 2 3 4 5
5. I have margin in my schedule for the unexpected.   1 2 3 4 5
6. I get a healthy amount of sleep and rest.   1 2 3 4 5
7. I take time to exercise and eat well to sustain my physical health.   1 2 3 4 5
8. I regularly devote time to my most important relationships.   1 2 3 4 5
9. I have a weekly sabbath practice that is restful and restorative.   1 2 3 4 5
10. I have a regular practice that helps me be God-conscious and self-aware.   1 2 3 4 5

Total: _____

SOUL ISSUES (GRATITUDE, TRUST AND CONTENTMENT)   1 2 3 4 5

1. I am grateful for all that has been given to me.   1 2 3 4 5
2. I celebrate and enjoy the abundance I've been given.   1 2 3 4 5
3. My life is largely free of fear, worry and anxiety.   1 2 3 4 5

4. I am happy when I see others enjoying their lives.   1 2 3 4 5

5. I rarely feel stressed out, tired or exhausted.   1 2 3 4 5

6. I am generally content with what I have.   1 2 3 4 5

7. I eat only as much as my body needs.   1 2 3 4 5

8. I don't struggle with being jealous of what others have. 1 2 3 4 5

9. Right now I have all that I need to be healthy and happy. 1 2 3 4 5

10. I believe that God will provide for my future needs.   1 2 3 4 5

Total: _____

MONEY MANAGEMENT

1. I have long-term financial goals.   1 2 3 4 5

2. I use a spending plan to budget my resources.   1 2 3 4 5

3. I have a strategy for managing cash, credit cards and bill
   payments that works well for me.   1 2 3 4 5

4. I only buy what I need.   1 2 3 4 5

5. I have a plan for eliminating or minimizing my debts.   1 2 3 4 5

6. I save part of my income for upcoming and unexpected expenses. 1 2 3 4 5

7. I give away a thoughtful percentage of my income.   1 2 3 4 5

8. I feel little stress about my financial situation.   1 2 3 4 5

9. My current spending and earning are sustainable.   1 2 3 4 5

10. I am able to talk openly and honestly about my finances. 1 2 3 4 5

Total: _____

ADDITIONAL QUESTIONS FOR COUPLES AND FAMILIES

11. My partner and I have mutually agreed upon an approach to how   1 2 3 4 5
    we budget and manage our finances.

12. My partner and I have a well negotiated understanding of who   1 2 3 4 5
    pays the bills, prepares taxes and records expenses.

13. I feel good about the values and skills I am teaching my kids about 1 2 3 4 5
    time, money and meaning.

Total: _____

GLOBAL SUSTAINABILITY

1. I have made conscious choices to limit my ecological footprint.	1 2 3 4 5
2. I have taken steps to lower my utility consumption.	1 2 3 4 5
3. I have taken steps to reduce packaging waste.	1 2 3 4 5
4. I recycle plastic, paper, glass and salvageable metals.	1 2 3 4 5
5. To reuse what's been made, I try to buy used items.	1 2 3 4 5
6. To avoid waste, I use reusable bags when I shop.	1 2 3 4 5
7. I walk, bike or use public transportation whenever possible.	1 2 3 4 5
8. I eat lower on the food chain by choosing less meat protein.	1 2 3 4 5
9. I buy local and organic goods whenever possible.	1 2 3 4 5
10. I buy products that were made justly and free of slave labor.	1 2 3 4 5

Total: _____

Look at your responses and calculate your totals for each category. In which areas did you have the highest total and strongest agreement? Circle your areas of strength:

Work and Meaning   Time Management   Soul Issues

Money Management   Global Sustainability

In your responses, where did you have the lowest total and least agreement? Circle your areas of growth:

Work and Meaning   Time Management   Soul Issues

Money Management   Global Sustainability

TASK: CHART YOUR DIRECTION FOR CHANGE

Pursuing a life of freedom and simplicity involves two important dimensions, vision and competency. To be fully alive and fruitful requires deepening your vision and values and cultivating practical skills. Most of us tend to be either vision-oriented (idealistic) or practical-minded (pragmatic), or sometimes we need to grow in both (striving). Knowing what your strengths are will help you identify the dimension you can lean toward to become more thriving. Which of the examples below do you most relate to?

Rachel has always been good at managing her money. She lives by a spending plan, gives generously and saves for long-term and upcoming expenses. But Rachel longs for change in how she spends her time. Her current job as a marketing director provides good benefits and financial stability, but doesn't reflect her deeper goals and values. She doesn't find her work particularly meaningful. Reflecting on her decision-making process, she realizes that she often makes her vocational choices based less on meaning and more on salary amount and benefits, reasoning that "a person with my skills and education should make X amount." She would like to take some risks to be more visionary in her work choices.

We might describe Rachel as pragmatic, high in financial competency but low in vision:

+ Skilled in earning and investing money

+ Competent with budgeting and financial management

+ Issue: time and finances not aligned with deeper vision and values

+ Direction for growth: Vertical. Making choices from a deeper sense of life purpose, vision and values

Diana, on the other hand, feels deeply passionate about her job as a social worker. When not at work she spends her time caring for friends or volunteering with organizations and causes she supports. Driven in her decisions by visionary ideals, she finds her life deeply meaningful. Yet Diana longs for change in how she manages her money. Although adequately paid, she has no reserve funds and has a large amount of credit card debt. Her financial situation creates anxiety for her. Gradually she has come to realize that it's time to balance her idealism with some practical financial skills and competencies. Diana is idealistic, high in vision and values but low in financial competency:

+ Lives from a deeper sense of life purpose

+ Makes conscious choices on behalf of others

→ Issue: Financial practices not aligned with deeper goals and values

→ Direction of growth: Horizontal. Develop earning, investing and budgeting skills

Ben and Amy have lived a life of urgency and striving ever since their son was born with a severe disability that requires constant care. Ben, who had no formal training, quickly took a course that qualified him for an entry-level position working with adults with disabilities. His job provides a modest income and much-needed health insurance, but his commute takes up two hours of each day. Amy supplements their income by running a beauty parlor out of their home. Their life often feels overwhelming, and in the rare moments when they have a break, it's easy to go out and spend money they don't have. Ben and Amy struggle to have a common vision for their lives and to make sense of their present circumstances. Life isn't what they thought it would be. Ben finds his job meaningful but would like to find better-paying work closer to home so he can be more available to care for his son. They would also like to get better at managing their money and paying off debts so they have more financial security. In their current situation Ben and Amy are striving, low in both vision and financial competency:

→ Making work and spending choices from an immediate sense of urgency

→ Struggling with basic financial competencies (earning and budgeting)

→ Issue: Unclear life vision and goals and difficulties with money management

→ Direction of growth: Diagonal. Clarify a deeper life purpose and develop financial skills

No matter where we begin, the goal for each of us is to move toward thriving, with highly developed vision and values and financial skills and competencies:

→ grateful, trusting, content and generous

→ financially sustainable

→ free to use time, talents and resources to pursue what matters most

→ making conscious and ethical spending choices that support global equity and ecological sustainability

> Looking at the "Direction of Change" figure, where would you place yourself? (Mark your place on the graph with a dot.)
>
> Which dimension would you like to grow toward? (Place an X and then draw an arrow from the dot to the X.)
>
> What advantages and challenges does your living context (urban, suburban or rural) offer that may shape your journey toward simplicity?

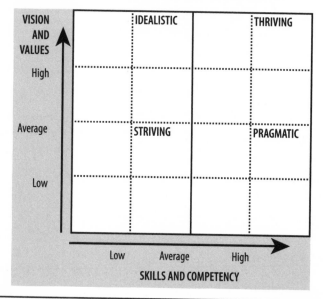

Direction of Change

1

Name What Matters Most to You

Seek first [God's] kingdom . . . and all these things will be given to you as well.

MATTHEW 6:33

Missy is one of our heroes, not because she is well known but for her hidden life of courage and beauty. We met when she was eleven years old, while Lisa and I were visiting families in a housing project where we organized a weekly kids' club. Tall for her age and extremely friendly, she quickly became a part of our lives, helping with kids' club, grocery shopping with Lisa or joining us for dinner at our apartment. Her home life was difficult. Dad was unemployed and battling drug and alcohol addictions. Mom was a survivor of abuse, and both parents struggled with bouts of explosive anger. The oldest of four children, Missy was more like a mother than a sister to her siblings. One day she told us that she needed a new Bible to replace the one we'd given her, explaining that she'd been reading it to the younger children as they fell asleep. It got soiled with urine when her younger brother, who has autism, wet the bed. When Missy was twelve, her dad lost control of his temper and struck her. After he was removed from the home, her mom invited a young man, later incarcerated for child sexual abuse, to live with the family.

Missy found a lot of comfort in the worship songs we sang at kids' club, and she asked me to teach her to play the guitar. We helped her buy a guitar, and once a week I would stop by to give a lesson, though we often ended up talking about her hurts, her concerns for her family or why God would allow these bad things to keep happening. When the house was loud and full of unsafe people, Missy would take the children upstairs and teach them the songs she had learned to play. Eventually she and her siblings were placed in foster care.

Despite the pain and obstacles she faced, Missy kept a strong faith in God, love for her family and a vision for her life. While most girls from the projects dropped out and had children before finishing high school, Missy stayed in school and in church, and eventually graduated from community college. She spent much of her early twenties working and volunteering with an early childhood education program in her neighborhood.

We've kept in touch over the years, and I recently asked Missy what matters most to her. She came back with a quick answer: God, my kids, my healing and my family. Missy has two children, Angel and Isaiah, ages six and seven. Both were diagnosed with severe autism spectrum disorder. Being the parent of a child with severe autism can be a delight, but it's not a life that most would choose. Many would say it's a life that is chosen for you. As a single parent, Missy's life is devoted to caring for her children's needs. In her words, "They consume most of my time, energy and intellect." Being a good parent to these children has many components: creating a calm environment, preparing a special diet, changing pull-ups, maintaining strict routines, practicing effective communication strategies and setting up twice-a-week in-home therapy sessions. She has to manage well the small amount of disability money she receives in order to pay her bills and provide her children with the specialized diet they require—a skill she has learned by necessity.

When I asked Missy what role God plays in her life, she said, "God? If I didn't have God in my life I wouldn't be able to do what I'm doing. He is working behind the scenes to help me." When her kids were diagnosed, she walked outside and shouted at the sky, "God, I can't do this. Why would you trust the most fragile kids in the world to me?" Missy says she heard a voice say, "I didn't give them to you so you can do this alone. You can rely on me." Having a conversational relationship with God helps her through the day.

Missy says that seeking healing is important to her because it helps her to become a better parent. "I have a lot of issues because of how I grew up. I have PTSD and dissociative disorder from the abuse I suffered. I also have a hard time setting healthy personal boundaries." She prays, journals and talks with friends, attends a church small group and is taking steps to exercise, eat better and get in shape. A fascinating turn of events is that her dad, who is now in recovery, has become a major source of support and spiritual strength. Looking back, Missy has many treasured memories of time with her mom making doll clothes, going on long walks and being taught to read. She believes her mom did the best she could and hopes that one day her mom can learn to "forgive and love on herself." Missy still plays an important role in her family as a daughter, a sister and a peacemaker.

Despite the incredible challenges she faces in life, Missy seeks to live from a deeper sense of vision and values, naming what matters most. We're inspired by her personal purpose statement: "Who I want to be is vastly different from who I am. But I will persevere. Not by my strength or abilities, but I will trust in God. I have to believe He made me for a special purpose, and it's ALWAYS too soon to quit!"

LIVING INTO THE QUESTIONS

It's never too late or too early to ask, Who am I and what do I want to be about? All the events of your life are conspiring to help you live into those questions. In the simplicity workshops that Lisa and I lead, whenever we ask participants to name what matters most to them, we are amazed by their quick responses. Though we may hesitate to voice the good dreams that are deep inside of us, they are often on the tip of our tongues:

"I want to work on behalf of women and children in the developing world."

"I love to solve problems and climb big mountains."

"I want to help those affected by human trafficking and extreme poverty."

"I love to make music."

"My dream might seem small, but I just want to have a good family. In the home I grew up in there was a lot of pain. I want to provide my kids with a safer and more loving environment."

Once during our workshop a woman began to cry. "I'm sad because I don't know what my purpose in life is!" she explained. "It's okay not to know," we replied. "If you don't feel like you know what your purpose in life is, maybe your purpose, at this point, is to search for the answer."

Thomas Merton suggests that although we instinctually know that life is meaningful, we don't know exactly what that meaning is. And so the task of our lives is to discover how life is meaningful. We may be tempted to settle for simplistic answers and miss it. Or we might be seduced to conclude that the answer is indiscernible and slip into despair. Merton suggests that it takes courage to continue to live into the questions.[1] In this chapter we are inviting you to live into four questions that will help you name what matters most to you:

1. What is my ultimate purpose?

2. Who am I?

3. What's right in front of me?

4. What will matter in the end?

---

[1] See the prologue to Thomas Merton, *No Man Is an Island* (Orlando: Mariner Books, 2002).

Some of us love to ponder the "big" questions. For others, those questions make our heads spin or seem removed from our everyday lives. We think naming what matters most involves asking larger top-down questions of meaning and paying attention to the bottom-up details of everyday life. The challenge for some of us is to connect our activities to a larger vision, and for others the challenge is to connect our big dreams to specific actions and tasks.

WHAT IS MY ULTIMATE PURPOSE?

The ancient Hebrews believed that the ultimate purpose of human life is expressed in the greatest command, in Jewish tradition called the Shema, which Jesus affirmed when he said that what matters most is to "love the Lord your God with all your heart and with all your soul and with all your mind and with all your strength. . . . [And to] love your neighbor as yourself" (Mark 12:30-31). Or as the prophet Micah put it,

He has shown you, O [people] what is good.
    And what does the LORD require of you?
To act justly and to love mercy
    and to walk humbly with your God. (Micah 6:8)

Jesus expanded on this with the revolutionary message that "the kingdom of God has come near" (Mark 1:15), affirming that our Creator is actively at work in our world bringing greater wholeness and restoration. Even more remarkable, Jesus believed that we can be agents of God's healing work in the world, which is evident from statements he made like "The kingdom of God is within you" (Luke 17:21 NIV 1984) and "Seek first [God's] kingdom" (Matthew 6:33). Paul the apostle echoed this same sentiment when he said, "We are God's handiwork, created . . . to do good" (Ephesians 2:10). This harkens back to the Genesis story in which Adam and Eve, as creatures made in the image of the invisible God, received the mandate to be good stewards of the creation (Genesis 1:26-28). The point seems to be that we can choose to live conscious of the fact that our actions matter and contribute to a larger story of God's dreams for our world.

In the garden, just before he was crucified, Jesus prayed, "This is eternal life: that they know you, the only true God, and Jesus Christ, whom you have sent" (John 17:3). Similarly, when Paul the apostle spoke in Athens, using philosophical language, he said,

> From one man [God] made every nation . . . that they should inhabit the whole earth; and [God] determined the times set for them and the exact places where they should live. God did this so that [people] would seek [God] and perhaps reach out for [God] and find [God], though [God] is not far from each one of us. "For in [God] we live and move and have our being." (Acts 17:26-28)

Elsewhere Paul states that his ultimate goal was to "know Christ" and the power of resurrection (Philippians 3:10). We're intrigued that the core of the Bible's message about our ultimate purpose isn't about doing or achieving. It's about relationship. Anyone, no matter what their age, or location in life, whether they are rich or poor, can pursue and experience what matters most—learning to live life with God. One way to summarize this is to say that our purpose is: to live with God and participate in the restorative activity of God in our world.

> *In one sentence, how would you summarize the ultimate purpose of human existence?*
>
> *Some people find it helpful to have a verse from Scripture that guides their life and decision making. If this is a meaningful activity for you, what verse would you choose?*

WHAT DOES IT LOOK LIKE FOR ME TO SEEK GOD'S KINGDOM?

In a big-picture sense we were made for relationship with God and one another, to enjoy life and to become good stewards of creation by seeking the greater good. But these ultimate statements of purpose don't address the everyday details of how you, specifically, are called to live out your purpose. This is why self-awareness is so important. A good question to ask is, Being the person that I am, in the time and place where I live, what does loving God and people look like for me?

That may be a question worth spending the rest of your life asking and striving to answer by the choices you make.

JOURNAL EXERCISE: WHO AM I?

It's never too late (or too soon) to think about who you are and to reflect on the good dreams that are deep inside of you. We find it helpful to spend some time considering these questions at least once a year. Take fifteen minutes to respond to the following questions.[2] You probably won't have to think that hard about these questions because what's most true about you is probably on the tip of your tongue. For each question write down the one or two things that come immediately to mind.

→ What am I passionate about? When do I feel most alive, vital, and energized? Your answer to these questions can help you identify the unique way that you were made to be of use in this world.

→ How would I describe my personality and temperament? Am I an introvert or extrovert? What core yearnings motivate my actions and decisions? When you are reflecting on your vision and goals, it is important to consider the gift and limits of your personality. You don't have to become someone else. Imagine scenarios that are realistic to who you were created to be.

→ Who is calling out the best in me? What do people recognize and affirm about my best contribution to the world? The feedback you receive from people who know you well can provide important clues about your destiny. If you aren't sure what people would say, ask them.

---

[2]These questions are taken from my book *Practicing the Way of Jesus* (Downers Grove, IL: InterVarsity Press, 2011), appendix one.

+ Who are the people in my life that are important for me to care for and journey with over my lifetime? This question acknowledges the fact that we are not meant to live as isolated individuals. Who are the stakeholders in your life (e.g., family, friends, a particular place and people)?

+ In what areas do I long for greater wholeness in my personal life? Each of us has wounds or struggles that we must face as we enter God's light more fully. Part of your journey as a person is discovering healing and finding ways to navigate your weaknesses.

+ Where do I sense the greatest need for justice and healing in our world? The struggles of suffering people, both locally and globally, can seem overwhelming. No one person can possibly carry all that pain. Each of us has been given sensitivity to a certain frequency of needs. What is breaking your heart that breaks the heart of God? Is it the physical needs of those in poverty; the emotional needs of those who are displaced, lonely or abused; the destruction of our natural resources; or something else?

+ What are my strongest talents, passions and skills? Where can they be of greatest service to others? You've been given skills, talents and expertise that can be leveraged for the good of the world. One of your primary life tasks is discerning how to best utilize these resources.

+ How does the work I presently do contribute to the greater good that God desires for our world? Although a worthy ambition, few of us get to do paid work that fully expresses all of our gifts and passions. But most jobs contribute something important to human society. School teachers help educate the next generation of citizens. Medical care providers support our physical health. Engineers and designers create products and structures to make our world safe, elegant and functional. Politicians, attorneys and law enforcement personnel create and enforce policies for the common good. Artists help us explore the wonder, beauty and terror of the human condition. How does the work you do bring good to the world?

WHAT MATTERS MOST TO YOU?

When Lisa and I began to consider getting married, I sought my dad's advice. He said, "Mark, you two are obviously in love with each other and a good match." What he said next surprised me: "But you should really take some time to figure out who you are and what you want to be about in life before you invite someone else into it."

Who are you and what do you want to be about?

When my father posed this, it came with a tinge of regret. When he was nineteen, he didn't know what he wanted to be about or even what he wanted to study in college. What he did know was that there was this girl (my mom) that he wanted to spend the rest of his life with, and that his relationship with God was important. My father came of age during the height of the Vietnam War, so his uncertainty about his future was partly answered by the draft. After marrying my mom he spent four years stationed in Germany with the US military. When he left the army he had two children to feed and took whatever work he could get. Although his life proved to be deeply meaningful, he wished he'd been more proactive about naming what mattered most to him earlier in life. He believed I had a chance to choose a path before it was chosen for me by the urgencies and circumstances of life.

Maybe it was the project management training he received in the military or just natural instinct, but Dad has always asked questions about what matters most and then set goals and made plans based on those goals. And he's still asking those questions with courage and ruthless self-examination. After years dominated by providing for a family and caring for aging parents, it took some time after retirement for the dreams and visions he'd left dormant to reawaken. At first he didn't quite know what to do with all the time on his hands. Gradually, he began investigating new interests and taking new risks. He spent eight months developing and teaching life skills classes at a local homeless shelter. He took time to deepen his spiritual life and tried new paths of prayer. Several days a week he enjoyed caring for his grandchildren. When a young, well-respected council person was tragically shot and killed in his city, Dad participated in demonstrations and started volunteering with a local peace activist group. He also began organizing neighborhood block parties to help build trust and safety among neighbors of many different ethnic backgrounds. Though he'd never been to the Two-Thirds World, he took the risk to participate in a serving trip to Haiti after the earthquake, where he worked with children in an orphanage. These experiences led to a deeper interest in crosscultural understanding and engagement. Recently, he began volunteering with a group that builds relationships with Muslim graduate students. Now serving as an elder in his church, he hopes to be an advocate for compassion, neighborhood engagement and cultural understanding.

TASK: CREATING A FIVE-WORD PURPOSE STATEMENT

Now that you've spent some time exploring and discerning who you are and what you were made to do, see if you can summarize that vision concisely using just five words. Use words that embody who you are and what you want your life to be about. For example, Lisa's five words are teacher, caregiver, maker, helper, friend. You might also find it helpful to create an "I statement" to go along with each of your words. The following are Mark's five words with "I statements":

Mystic: I want to live in awareness and surrender to my Creator.

Lover: I want to be a caring and connected husband, father, son and friend.

Artist: I want to explore and express the wonder, beauty and terror of life.

Teacher: I want to help people experience transformation through active learning.

Healer: I want to be a friend to those who struggle and work on behalf of those who suffer.

Notice that this purpose statement doesn't directly address questions of job or career goals. That's because a purpose statement is intended to highlight deeper values of identity that might be expressed in a variety of paid or unpaid roles. Discerning who you are and what you are truly after in life is more important and enduring than any role or position you might have.

If you had to capture who you are and what you are about in five words with "I statements" what would you write?

_____: I want to _____

_____: I want to _____

_____: I want to _____

_____: I want to _____

_____: I want to _____

Once you have developed your purpose statement, you can use it to help you find meaning in your current activities. "I'm caring for this child because family is important to me." Or "I'm answering this email because it's part of my work as a maker to bring good to the world." You can also use your purpose statement to help you make clear choices when presented with new opportunities. "Does this fit with my deeper values and sense of identity?" Your purpose statement is a tool to help you make good decisions about your time and money. It's not intended to be a list of rules. Expect your purpose statement to shift or become more focused over time.

If you are part of a family, you may also want to create a family purpose statement to help guide your decision making. Here's our family purpose statement:

Know and love God.

Nurture and care for one another.

Offer hospitality.

Care for people with struggles.

Live creatively and use our gifts to serve others.

Live a life of gratitude and simplicity.

Noticing Your Children
Lisa Scandrette

How can you help a child discover his or her purpose in the world? I believe it begins with noticing who the child is—including personality, strengths and interests—and affirming that God made him or her to be a good person. Notice what the child gravitates toward. What can you expose the child to? What experiences can you offer the child that may ignite his or her interest or passion? Each child has God-given gifts that can be cultivated for the good of others.

One of our children loves to explain things. In fact, one of his first words was the word *actually*. As he's grown, we've looked for healthy ways for him to explore this passion for knowing and telling. When he was twelve, he was asked to assist in helping to teach five- and six-year-olds in a nature studies class. In high school he has worked at a science museum, explaining exhibits to the public and how various scientific demonstrations work. This summer he helped kids in East Oakland document where they see God's beauty in their neighborhood through photography. Our hope is that as he has had the opportunity to experience different ways of teaching and explaining, he might have a better idea of the sorts of things that he is made to do and even some of the things that he is not made to do.

You can open doors for a child by connecting them with people and situations that inspire them. Show the child how he or she might do good in the world. Let the child see places where the world aches for the touch of God. Perhaps he or she will be drawn to do something. Support the child and help them make their good ideas happen.

WHAT'S RIGHT IN FRONT OF ME?

What is the meaning of life? The ancient philosopher of Ecclesiastes went on a daring quest to discover the answer to this question. He trained in scholarly wisdom, acquired wealth and power, and pursued sensual pleasures, denying nothing his "eyes desired" (Ecclesiastes 2:10). He discovered that life cannot be any more meaningful than it already is. If you strive too hard, you will miss it. True meaning is found in the details: enjoying our food, our work and our closest relationships, and being conscious of the ultimate reality who gave us life as a gift and sacred trust. In fact striving and discontent are what can make life seem meaninglessness. His conclusion was:

> A person can do nothing better than to eat and drink and find satisfaction in their toil. This too, I see, is from the hand of God, for without him, who can eat or find enjoyment? To the person who pleases him, God gives wisdom, knowledge and happiness, but to the sinner he gives the task of gathering and storing up wealth to hand it over to the one who pleases God. This too is meaningless, a chasing after the wind. (Ecclesiastes 2:24-26)

We often set goals with the hope that what we wish to achieve or acquire will make our lives more meaningful or fulfilling. Our goals can be a not-so-subtle expression of discontent: I'll be happy when . . . I'm married . . . I own a home . . . I have a child . . . I have gotten my dream job . . . I've gone on my dream vacation . . . or I've achieved an important milestone in my career. The truth is that right now you have everything you need to have a meaningful and fulfilling life. Perhaps the greatest goal you could have in life is to more deeply embrace the life you've been given—your work, your relationships, your enjoyment of life's simple pleasures and your awareness of the sacred. This was what the wise teacher of Ecclesiastes repeated:

> Go, eat your food with gladness, and drink your wine with a joyful heart, for God has already approved what you do. Always

be clothed in white, and always anoint your head with oil. Enjoy life with your wife, whom you love, all the days of this meaningless life that God has given you under the sun—all your meaningless days. For this is your lot in life and in your toilsome labor under the sun. Whatever your hand finds to do, do it with all your might. (Ecclesiastes 9:7-10)

TASK: CREATE ONE-YEAR GOALS IN KEY LIFE AREAS

How do you want to more deeply embrace the life you've been given? Consider the basic aspects of your life: your physical health, your relationships, the work of your hands, your soul care and emotional well-being, and the simple pleasures of life that you enjoy. We can set goals in each of these areas to deepen our experience of and satisfaction with the lives we've been given. For each area, consider how you would like to deepen your experience of that aspect of your life over the next year by taking three to five concrete steps of action.

Body care. What is your goal for physical health and well-being? Use an I statement like, "I would like to have more energy and maintain a healthy weight."

_____

_____

What are three to five steps that support this goal? Examples: Eat more fruits and vegetables. Exercise four to five times a week. Get at least seven hours of sleep per night.

1._____

2._____

3._____

4._____

5._____

What are the time or financial considerations are related to taking these steps? Examples: Buy new running shoes. Go to the farmers' market every Saturday.

_____

_____

Relationships. You are connected to family, friends, coworkers and neighbors. How would you like to see these relationships made deeper or stronger? What goals do you have for your most important relationships?

_____

_____

What are three to five steps that support this goal? Examples: Go on a weekly date with my partner. Call my parents/siblings once a month. Eat dinner with my family/housemates.

1._____

2._____

3._____

4._____

5._____

What are the time or financial considerations related to taking these steps? Examples: Set aside time and funds for weekly dates. Schedule a visit to my grandmother and save up travel money.

_____

_____

The work of your hands. How does the work you do, whether paid or unpaid, provide for needs, serve others, express your gifts and contribute to the greater good of God's kingdom? What are your goals for the work that you do?

_____

_____

What are three to five steps that support this goal? Examples: Pray daily for my boss and co-workers. Make a list of priorities for each day of work. Get a journal article published. Look for a job that better fits my deeper passions.

1._____

2._____

3._____

4._____

5._____

What are the time or financial considerations related to taking these steps? Examples: Set aside funds to take a computer skills class. Schedule time off to work on my dissertation.

_____

_____

Soul care. You were created to live in reverence and grateful awareness of your Maker. What are your goals for deepening your connection to the sacred and being emotionally healthy and centered?

_____

_____

What are three to five steps that support this goal? Examples: Set aside thirty minutes a day for meditation and prayer. Take an annual silent retreat. Go on a weekly hike with a supportive friend.

1._____
2._____
3._____
4._____
5._____

What are the time or financial considerations related to taking these steps? Examples: Set aside funds to stay at retreat center. Leave work promptly at 5 p.m.

_____

_____

Rest and play. This might include things like food, nature, hobbies and culture. What helps you relax and experience what we've been given to enjoy? What is your goal for enjoying the simple pleasures of life?

_____

_____

What are the three to five steps that support this goal? Examples: Cook food for friends. Go fishing. Visit an art museum. Watch a football game. Knit a sweater.

1._____
2._____
3._____
4._____
5._____

What are the time or financial considerations related to taking these steps? Examples: Budget funds for craft supplies. Buy a museum membership. Reserve one day a week for recreation.

Don't feel like this exercise is once and for all time. As you learn and grow, your values and goals may shift, change or become more clearly defined. That's why it's a good idea to check in on your values and goals once a month, and reevaluate them each year—and especially at every new life stage (or about every five years).

WHAT WILL MATTER IN THE END?

I once asked my grandfather if he had any advice for me after living for so many years. "Don't get old," he replied with a smirk. I remember visiting him in the care facility where he lived during his last days. After my grandmother passed away and the possessions of their house had been sold or given away, all that he owned fit in a single room in a few dresser drawers. No one at the care facility could fully appreciate who this man was—that he'd been a distinguished college professor, an accomplished photographer or that before he'd lost his speech he was an exceptional storyteller. The achievements of his life were now in the past and largely forgotten. On a crumpled piece of paper my grandfather kept a penciled list of articles he'd written for popular magazines and academic journals, the last evidence of the accomplishments of his life. He would hand me the piece of paper and point at the list, as if to say, "See who I was and what I've done." That image has stuck with me.

Thinking about the end can help bring what matters into focus. For my grandfather it came down to the love and care of his family, the comfort of praying the Psalms and the simple pleasure of a short walk through the turning leaves of fall. In an article titled "Regrets of the Dying," Bronnie Ware reports the top five regrets of the patients she worked with during the years she provided palliative care:

→ I wish I'd had the courage to live a life true to myself, not the life others expected of me.

→ I wish I didn't work so hard.

→ I wish I'd had the courage to express my feelings.

→ I wish I'd stayed in touch with my friends.

→ I wish that I had let myself be happier.[3]

How sad to consider that so many of us spend our lives the way we thought we should live, rather than in a way that is truly fulfilling. Thinking toward the future can help us clarify our deeper life purpose and goals.

JOURNAL EXERCISE: IMAGINING THE FUTURE

Imagine you reach the ripe old age of eighty-five in good health and of sound mind. How do you hope to look? Who do you hope to spend your time with? What do you imagine you will do with your time? What will you look back on with gratitude and satisfaction?

When you are considering what matters most to you, it can also help to think about the fact that you are going to die. "Teach us to number our days, that we may gain a heart of wisdom" (Psalm 90:12). Someday your body will be laid in a coffin. What do you hope the people closest to you might say at your funeral? What kind of obituary will they write for the local newspaper?

If contemplating your death seems a bit too morbid, what are some pictures you see of yourself in the less distant future? These pictures can be a powerful tool for helping you decide what's important.

---

[3]Bronnie Ware, "Regrets of the Dying," *Inspiration and Chai,* accessed December 5, 2012, http://inspirationandchai.com/Regrets-of-the-Dying.html.

Do you find it exciting or challenging to think about larger questions of vision and purpose? Why?

Which exercise was the most interesting or had the most impact on you? Explain.

What new insights or questions came up for you when you were doing these exercises?

What surprised you about your responses?

2

Value and Align Your Time

There is a time for everything,
and a season for every activity under the heavens:
a time to be born and a time to die,
a time to plant and a time to uproot,
a time to kill and a time to heal,
a time to tear down and a time to build,
a time to weep and a time to laugh,
a time to mourn and a time to dance,
a time to scatter stones and a time to gather them,
a time to embrace and a time to refrain from embracing,
a time to search and a time to give up,
a time to keep and a time to throw away,
a time to tear and a time to mend,
a time to be silent and a time to speak,
a time to love and a time to hate,
a time for war and a time for peace.

ECCLESIASTES 3:1-8

*B*ring up the subject of time in almost any group and you are likely to get a variety of impassioned responses about busyness, regrets or competing demands. Most of us have charged emotions or insecurities about how we spend our time. Which of these feelings about time do you most relate to?

→ I feel hurried and tired.

→ I feel peaceful and content with how I spend my time.

→ I don't have enough time.

→ I should be getting more done than I am.

→ I feel expectations and demands on my time from others.

→ I fear that I'm wasting my time.

→ I wonder whether I'm getting to what's really important.

In our culture people regularly comment on how busy they are—often with the underlying assumption that busyness somehow equals success or importance. Those of us who are less busy may feel subtle pressure to fill our time with more activities. But the fact is, we all have the same amount of time. We simply make different choices about how we spend it.

Our feelings and decisions are influenced by the underlying messages we believe about time. Which of these common messages do you most identify with?

→ Success won't come if I don't work harder than everyone else.

→ If people don't see what I do, they won't think I'm important.

→ If my kids aren't in a lot of activities, they'll fall behind and have less opportunities.

→ If I say no to an opportunity, I might miss out.

→ If I say yes, I'm afraid I'll be overwhelmed.

→ I like to feel needed, so I have a hard time saying no.

+ I put very little on my schedule because I need to feel safe and in control.

+ I'd rather distract myself with activity than face the real issues and tasks of my life.

+ I want to maximize my time so I schedule as much as I possibly can.

+ If I were doing something different than I am right now, I would be happier.

+ My life would be better now if I'd made different choices earlier.

Many of us live with regrets about missed opportunities and unfulfilled dreams. Which of those dreams are true to the nature of who you are, and which of those dreams are whims that it's okay to lay aside because they were never meant to be? Who of us hasn't thought that another place or another job would be the perfect container of our hopes and dreams—only to discover that we bring ourselves, what we are trying to escape, to that next place? Even the most meaningful and vital work can feel mundane in the day-to-day meetings, appointments, email and expense reports. It can be tempting to imagine how great someone else's life must be or dwell on how your life must look to others. What matters is how your life feels from the inside, how you experience it. Sometimes the deeper work is within, finding meaning in the everyday details and coming to a place of peace and contentment with the life you have received.

LIVING IN TIME WITH PRESENCE AND PURPOSE

Observing our collective frustrations with time, the ancient philosopher wrote, "I have seen the burden God has laid on the human race. He has made everything beautiful in its time. He has also set eternity in the human heart; yet no one can fathom what God has done from beginning to end" (Ecclesiastes 3:10-11). Our relationship with time involves both how we spend it and how we experience it. To value and align your time requires learning to live in time with presence and purpose.

Jesus modeled an intriguing perspective on time, which is captured in a particular incident. During an important feast when many would be gathered, Jesus' brothers encouraged him to appear publicly. Essentially they told him, "If you want to be famous, you need to show up at this event." Notice how Jesus responds and what this reveals about his perspective on time and significance: "My time is not yet here; for you any time will do. The world cannot hate you, but it hates me because I testify that its works are evil. You go to the festival. I am not going up to this festival, because my time has not yet fully come" (John 7:6-8).

For Jesus time was not only chronological, it involved a kairos moment or right opportunity. One of the more challenging observations we've heard philosopher Dallas Willard make is that Jesus was never in a hurry, he was always on time and prepared to do what was being asked of him by the Father. Willard suggests that we can take from this that there are always enough hours in the day for what God requires of us. If we can't get through the activities of our day without feeling rushed or hurried, then we are probably trying to do more than what God asks of us. Though intent on fulfilling his purpose, Jesus was never in a hurry and knew that his time would come. For those who strive, it's hard to believe that there really is "a time for everything" (Ecclesiastes 3:1). Perhaps our hurry and busyness come from not being clear about what our purpose is. When you don't know what you are about, you'll say yes to anything, anxious to fill the void with activity. Those who are clear about their purpose are able to rest and live deliberately, free of hurry and striving.

BEING WATCHFUL AND PRESENT

One of the main spiritual disciplines regarding time is learning to be present to your life in this moment, recognizing that you are alive and that God is with you. The apostle Paul suggests that God "marked out [our] appointed times in history and the boundaries of [our] lands. God did this so that [we] would seek him and perhaps reach out for him and find him, though he is not far from any one of us. 'For in him we live and move and have our being'" (Acts 17:26-28). With the noise, speed and distractions of contemporary society, it's not surprising that silence, solitude and contemplative prayer have emerged as such important and transformative practices for many.

EXPERIMENT: BE STILL

Try this. Set aside this book for five minutes. Close your eyes, breathe deeply and simply sit. What do you notice? What do you hear? What do you smell? How does your body feel? In the absence of activity, what are you drawn to think about? What kind of thoughts come to the surface? Can you let go of those thoughts to be still and know that God is here and that you are alive in this moment?

As a way to reset a sense of restful presence, many people find it helpful to have a daily or regular practice of stillness prayer—five, ten or twenty minutes of focused silence to be aware of God and be present to yourself. As an experiment you may want to practice this kind of stillness for a period of time each day for a week to see how it subtly shifts your sense of time, hurry or anxiety.[1]

EXPERIMENT: LIMIT THE PLACE OF MEDIA IN YOUR LIFE

For many of us the pervasiveness of technology and social media has intensified the challenge to be at rest in our activities. Smart phones, social networking and email, when not used consciously, can keep us in a constant state of distraction. Many people find it helpful to experiment with abstaining from media or setting limits on their daily use of technology. For example, no email before 8 a.m. or after 6 p.m. Try fasting from social networking, the Internet, TV and music for

---

[1]For a more thorough exploration of this practice see chapter seven of *Practicing the Way of Jesus* (Downers Grove, IL: InterVarsity Press, 2011).

one week. An experiment like this can help you establish a baseline for the effect that constant media may have in your life.

SABBATH

> Six days you shall labor and do all your work, but the seventh day is a sabbath to the LORD your God. On it you shall not do any work, neither you, nor your son or daughter, nor your male or female servant, nor your animals, nor any foreigner residing in your towns. For in six days the LORD made the heavens and the earth, the sea, and all that is in them, but he rested on the seventh day. Therefore the LORD blessed the Sabbath day and made it holy. (Exodus 20:9-11)

Since ancient times, people in many faith traditions have found it helpful to observe a weekly day of rest. In Judeo-Christian tradition it is one of the Ten Commandments. In his teachings Jesus clarified that "the Sabbath was made to meet the needs of people, and not people to meet the requirements of the Sabbath" (Mark 2:27 NLT). Traditionally, sabbath is a break from all productive labor, which provides rest for all people and animals, regardless of social status. These and other dimensions of sabbath call into question the 24/7 manic production tendencies of our culture.

Sabbath is a time to remember that we are creatures who receive life as a gift. It gives us a chance to rest from work, celebrate life and reflect on who we are as beings living in God's world. Though it's easy to approach sabbath with a list of dos and don'ts, we find it most helpful to enter sabbath by asking, "What will make this day the most restorative for me and distinctive in pace and activities from the other six days of the week?" It is even better if your sabbath practice doesn't require anyone else to work. A restful sabbath will include activities you intentionally engage in and abstain from. For example, because I use my phone and computer for work, for me, sabbath is about taking a break from email and text messaging. My work also involves many meetings and social events, so for me, sabbath is a time when I don't plan any social obligations outside of time with my family.

EXPERIMENT: SABBATH KEEPING

Practice a twenty-four-hour sabbath that is restful, restorative and gives you opportunity to "pamper your soul." Use the following questions to help you think through what a restorative sabbath practice might be for you and the people you share life with, and schedule twenty-four hours for sabbath this week.

→ What are some activities that you find restorative? Examples: taking a nap, being out in nature, visiting a museum, reading a good book.

→ What are the normal activities (and obligations) you do during the week that you would like to abstain from to make the sabbath a distinctive day of space, rest and reflection?

→ What kind of preparations do you need to make in order to stop working for twenty-four hours? Examples: shop and prepare food ahead of time, shut down the computer, tidy the house so that it's a place where you feel comfortable relaxing.

→ During what twenty-four hours will you practice sabbath this week? It doesn't have to be on a Saturday or Sunday and could start at any time of the day.

ALIGNING YOUR TIME WITH YOUR DEEPER VALUES AND GOALS

Your time is your life. How you spend your time is how you spend your life. Perhaps this is why the apostle Paul admonished his readers, "Be careful how you live. Don't live like fools, but like those who are wise. Make the most of every opportunity" (Ephesians 5:15-16 NLT). Time is one of the main currencies of our lives. Your calendar is a reflection of what truly matters to you—not what you say matters to you. As beings made in the image of an intelligent Creator, we have the incredible capacity to decide where to direct our life energy. We are invited to be intentional about how we use our time. Though there are a nearly infinite number of things you could do with your time, you can't do them all. You have to choose what is most important. One key spiritual discipline you can practice is aligning your time with your deeper values and goals. Creating and enacting a time budget can be a helpful tool for practicing this discipline.

Stronger and More Connected
Hailey Scandrette

I'm still finding my own path for living simply and spending my time and money on what matters most, but I find that identifying and attempting to live out my values make me feel stronger as a person and more connected to the world around me. Living in a simple way means that I'm free to invest my time and money in things that I feel are important. I have money to donate to causes that resonate with me, and I have time to volunteer at a local theater helping with their kids' programs. Right now I'm leading a book club for some of my younger "theater sisters." When I was in my early teens, my book club was a very formative and welcoming place for me. Setting aside time to provide other girls that kind of environment feels important to me. For me making time for what matters can be as small as taking a friend out to coffee because she's having a bad week or taking time to write your dad a note because he's hopping on a plane at 5 a.m. tomorrow and you know it will make him smile. ;)

TASK: CREATE A TIME BUDGET

You can use the time budgeting worksheets at the end of this chapter (see figs. 2.1-2.4) to help you work through the following steps for creating a time budget that values and aligns your time with what matters most to you.

Step 1. Estimate your current use of time. Using the one-year goals you developed in key life areas in chapter one, estimate the number of hours per day and per week that you currently spend on body care, relationships, the work of your hands, soul care, and rest and play. This is an estimate of how you are currently using your time, not necessarily how you would like to be spending your time. After completing your time estimate consider:

→ What stood out to you? Were there any surprises in where your time is going?

→ Which activities do you want to spend more time on as a reflection of your deeper values and goals?

→ What do you think you will have to say no to in order to align your time with what matters most?

→ What do you hear the Spirit nudging you toward in regard to how you spend your time?

Step 2. Align your time with your purpose statement and goals. Look at the purpose statement and goals you developed in chapter one. Does the way you are currently using your time support the deeper goals and values you've identified? For each category in your time budget, determine whether you need to spend more or less time in that category to support your deeper values and goals, or if the time you spend should remain the same. For instance, you might decide that you are spending too much time at work and not enough time with your family or other important relationships. Or you might decide that you would like to spend more time on your physical health and soul care. Write down how much time you can realistically afford to spend in each category on a daily and weekly basis.

Here are a few questions and factors to consider as you go through this process.

Body care. Sleep is one of the most important ways that you can care for your physical health. How many hours of sleep do you usually get? How many hours do you need to be fully rested and prepared for the day? At what time would you need to get up and go to bed in order to get this amount of sleep?

The work of your hands. Although we might naturally think of paid work as the work of our hands, there are other kinds of work that are part of our lives, including household chores and unpaid service. The value of our unpaid work is just as important as the work we are paid to do. Many of the most important jobs in our society are done by unpaid volunteers and are difficult to quantify monetarily: parenting the next generation well, being a good neighbor, caring for the elderly and those at risk. When we do pay people to perform these caregiving roles, it can be very expensive. Consider these questions about your paid and unpaid work:

→ In what way does the work you do contribute to the good of the world?

→ What skills, talents and passions does your work allow you to express?

→ Would you do your current job even if you weren't paid to or didn't need the money?

→ What kind of work do you dream about doing someday? Are you taking steps toward that work right now? What's holding you back?

→ What are the chores you do on a daily or weekly basis to maintain your household? Examples: grocery shopping, cooking, washing, cleaning, walking the dog, managing finances, yard work, home maintenance and repairs.

→ What volunteer service do you provide for your family, neighborhood and community? Examples: caring for children or older relatives, serving in your neighborhood or at your church, using your skills and talents as a volunteer.

Soul care. List the regular practices that help keep your mind and spirit sustained. Examples: prayer, meditation, church participation, AA, seeing a therapist.

Rest and play. List what you typically do or would like to do to unwind and relax at the end of the day or on weekends, vacations and holidays.

Step 3. Build in margin and boundaries. The ancient Hebrews were invited into a way of life that had space and margin. Every week had a sabbath (Exodus 20:10) and every seven years the land was to have rest—a year without sowing and reaping (Leviticus 25:4). Every fifty years all debts were to be forgiven and land returned to its original owners (Leviticus 25:10). Though it's debatable whether the Israelites consistently practiced this way of life, it's inspiring to consider the spacious, restful pace of life they were invited into. Imagine how most of us would have to rearrange our finances in order to take a year off from work every seven years, or how our economy would need to shift if we calculated debts in terms of a jubilee year. In Hebrew tradition it was common practice to leave the edges of fields unharvested for immigrants and the poor to glean from (Leviticus 19:9). The invitation seemed to be into a life with space and margin—and away from a life of striving to maximize the productivity and profit of every moment and piece of property.

What might it look like for you to make more space for life? As you create your time budget, consider leaving margin and establishing the boundaries needed to make your life more sustainable. Some activities and tasks inevitably take longer than anticipated, or our plans are delayed because of a sickness, traffic or an unexpected opportunity to care for someone in need. Leaving space allows for the unpredictable and will help you to live without hurry.

When creating your time budget you may also want to consider your energy level at certain times of the day or week. When are you the most alert? When do you feel the most tired? We've learned, for instance, not to schedule meetings or difficult conversations on Friday nights, which is the time of the week when we are the most tired.

EXERCISE: IDENTIFYING YOUR TIME BANDITS

We all have time bandits, activities that take more of our time than we estimate or plan for. It could be that one-hour lunch with a friend that ends up being three hours, the extra time at work that adds up to a day a week, or that hour of TV, Internet or video games that turns into a whole evening. We're not suggesting that these are unhelpful activities in themselves, but they become time bandits if they don't actually provide what we need or distract us from what is more important.

First, make a list of your time bandits. Then consider a strategy or boundary you would like to put in place to help you keep your time priorities.

The following are a few ideas for setting time boundaries:

With media. We have found the following strategies helpful for managing our media use.

→ Decide how much time you want to spend on the activity before you begin.

→ Make it contingent on finishing more important activities. For example, "I can watch TV after I exercise and clean the house."

→ Remind yourself of other ways you find rest, and try one of those first. Go for a walk. Take a bath. Read. Go to bed.

Many people have also found it helpful to set voluntary limits and boundaries to their use of technological devices.

→ Only check email at the beginning and end of each day or, if you can, just once or twice a week.

→ Turn phone off while meeting with people and during family times.

→ Set boundaries on the time of day and number of hours when you use the computer or sit in front of screens.

→ Have a media-free day of the week—a sabbath.

With work. Our work can be managed more effectively by following two simple strategies.

→ Do the most important tasks first.

→ Some people find it helpful to set a limit on the number of hours to work; this limit makes them more focused and productive.

With people. For some of us, setting boundaries in our time with people can also be an important practice.

→ Let the person know ahead of time how much time you have.

→ Learn a few helpful phrases like, "I can't. I have an appointment." That appointment could be time to yourself or space to accomplish something on your to-do list.

→ Prioritize your relationships.

Due to social networking and increasing mobility, many of us know and have connections with more people than we can possibly maintain consistent relationships with. Trying to keep up all of these relationships can make life feel crazy—or we feel guilty for not staying in better contact. Many people find it helpful to prioritize their relationships by deciding who to spend time with first. This practice might not fit everyone's situation or might seem relationally risky, but for those of us who struggle with overcommitment, it can be an important step to sanity. Our friend Chris says,

> Time has become a most valuable commodity for me—so who I spend my time with is just as important as how I spend my time. Relationships are a driving force in who I am. Where I spend the precious hours I have outside of work and family are an important reflection of my values. I give priority to those who really know me, who are life-giving and supportive companions on the journey or who need my help. It isn't that I don't occasionally hang out with those not in my inner circle, but my priority is with these core relationships. A friend to all is a friend to none.

Step 4. Balance your time budget. Add up the total number of hours per day and week you've proposed in each category, allowing for some margin. Does it all fit? Or do you need to adjust your activities? Do you have an hour or two of margin in your day to account for interruptions and some activities taking longer than you anticipated?

Step 5. Consider tradeoffs. Decide whether there are any tradeoffs that might help you spend more of your time on what you believe matters most.

A few years ago while meeting with a young man who came to me for spiritual direction, he happened to mention how much money he earned a year. Surprised at the amount I said, "Wow, that's a lot more than I make, and I'm much older than you!" He quickly replied, "Yes, but you love what you do. I spend the better part of my days doing something I find meaningless and trivial."

There are costs to the choices we make, and these often include tradeoffs between time, money and meaning. Which is most valuable? It really depends on what seems more scarce. In our society many of us have more money than time or meaningful activities and relationships. Though many families benefit from having both parents work, often the economic advantages of having two full-time incomes are diminished by increased expenses: higher taxes, childcare and commuter costs, work wardrobe, and a tendency to spend more for convenience due to a lack of time. It is often suggested that many of our common problems, including depression and obesity, are related to the levels of stress we feel and the demands and expectations on our time. Typically, we seek solutions to these and other struggles through therapists, doctors, medications, vacations or luxury comforts. In some cases a more effective solution might be to adopt a simpler lifestyle and slower pace of life.

Sometimes the tradeoffs can be navigated with incremental changes like a few less hours at work or more evenings at home. And at other times, a more dramatic shift may be required to get the freedom you want to pursue what matters most.

In the Bay Area where we live, it's not uncommon for people to commute two to four hours roundtrip to work each day. Even though Ryan's job was in Silicon Valley, he and his wife Jen reasoned that the only way they could raise a family was to live in Tracy, California, where they could afford a new 3,200-square-foot home. Every morning Ryan left at 4:40 a.m. to get to his office in Cupertino by 8:00 a.m. On most days he would arrive home from work at 7:30 or 8:00 p.m., hopefully in time to see their two preschool children for a few minutes before they went off to bed. Exhausted by work and his long commute, Ryan would try to relax with a big meal before falling asleep in front of the TV. On the weekends he would try to catch up on missed opportunities with the family. They would attempt to do something memorable and special, which often involved spending money on restaurants, expensive toys like a speed boat or ski weekends in Tahoe. The family rarely went to church or connected with friends because Ryan was too tired or the family needed to catch up on chores that had been neglected during the week. Feeling the strain in their relationship after several years of this lifestyle, Ryan and Jen couldn't take it any longer. They began examining the tradeoffs between time and money, and decided to make some dramatic changes. They decided that the core of their problem was Ryan's commute. There were few jobs in Ryan's field in Tracy, so that meant relocating to Silicon Valley, where housing was three times the cost. To make the move they would have to downsize from a spacious home with four bedrooms and a three-car garage to a modest two-bedroom condominium. But their new home was only ten minutes from Ryan's office. He was now able to eat breakfast with the family and return home by 6:00 p.m. every night. What they gave up in square footage they gained in family life—and they even had time to see friends, join a church and serve in their community.

Recent research regarding commute times, economics and well-being suggests that if your commute is an hour each way, you have to make 40 percent more to make up for misery and lost time. Most long-range commuters make their daily treks, even when it's clearly demonstrated that the time they're spending on the road or train has no economic advantages. Researchers concluded that we don't always do things because they make sense but by force of habit. It's easier to keep doing what we do, even if it's killing us, than to risk making new decisions.[2]

> *What are the tradeoffs you are making between money and time?*
>
> *Do you need to give up some time to earn more money, or would you like to earn less to spend more time doing what matters most to you?*
>
> *Are you happy with the tradeoffs, or would you like to make different choices?*

TASK: ENACT YOUR TIME BUDGET

The final step to creating a time budget is using tools to implement the priorities you've established.

Calendar your time. The most important moments in our lives don't happen by accident. If we leave them up to chance, they get crowded out by other activities or priorities. Looking back at your target time priorities, plot out a weekly and monthly schedule, using either a paper or electronic calendar.

Establish predictable rhythms. One of the best tools for enacting your deeper values and priorities is working them into regular rhythms of life. We believe it's helpful to plan in terms of daily, weekly, yearly and seasonal rhythms. This means choosing a regular time to do the things that are important to you. For instance, Lisa and I have a weekly date time. For most of the seasons of our family we've had a family night, a family sabbath day and weekly dad and kid dates. We also schedule rhythms for physical exercise, volunteering, silent retreats, vacations and visiting relatives. As human beings we crave and were made to live within rhythms. If most of your schedule is flexible and you practice moment-by-moment decision making, it will be harder to sustain in-

---

[2]See Alois Stutzer and Bruno S. Frey, "Stress That Doesn't Pay: The Commuting Paradox," *Scandinavian Journal of Economics* 110, no. 2 (2008): 339-66, doi:10.1111/j.1467-9442.2008.00542.x.

tentionality. Even when a person doesn't have an intentional rhythm, an unintentional rhythm or repeated pattern often develops. By establishing sustaining rhythms you can make what's most important a habit.

Have a weekly planning meeting. Once a week, usually on Sundays, we have a weekly meeting to review our schedules for the upcoming week, examine our goals and have ongoing conversations about finances, household chores, family life, our relationships and personal growth. In the weekly meeting we look at the calendar for the week and month ahead, and review the opportunities that have come up. Some might think that this is too formal or businesslike for handling a personal or family schedule. But your life is so important, why wouldn't you treat it with the same intentionality as you would if you were running a business? We've found that when we skip too many weekly meetings, we tend to get busier and our priorities become fuzzy.

Set daily priorities. Many people find it helpful at the beginning of the day to look over their schedule and decide what the most important tasks of the day are. As you probably know, it's a good practice to do what's most important first.

Make decisions about new opportunities. Not all of life fits neatly into a calendar and schedule. New invitations and opportunities come up regularly. You may find it helpful to use the following questions to guide your decisions:

+ Does it fit with my values and goals?

+ What is it going to take the place of?

+ Is this better or best?

+ What do I hear the inner voice of the Spirit saying to me about this opportunity?

Revisit your priorities yearly. Once a year Lisa and I set aside two or three hours to reflect on the previous year and set goals for the following year. We look at whether we reached the goals we set out to achieve; we make a list of what was good and what was difficult about the year. Then we brainstorm what we would like to be different in the future and come up with four or five major goals for the year. For instance, we might have had a very full year and decide the following year needs to be more quiet and have more space. Or we might anticipate needing to do some repair work on our house, so we might schedule less weekend activities. Or we recognize that our family is entering a new season of life that will require a new weekly rhythm.

When we first started creating time budgets for ourselves we could stick to the budget for just a few weeks before neglecting or abandoning it. Maybe you can relate to our frustration. We were a bit idealistic and didn't allow enough margin or account for our varying levels of energy. Learning to use time well requires patience, practice and growing self-awareness. We rarely get this stuff completely dialed in, or as soon as we think we have, a new season of life begins. This is something we keep going back to, improvising and playing with. It's a dance that hopefully we get better at with time.

RISK BEING FULLY ALIVE

It's possible that in working through the process of creating a time budget, you realize that your current commitments are limiting your ability to pursue what matters most to you. It might be time for a dramatic change. Some of us have a hard time saying no, but some of us have a hard time saying yes and stepping up to the challenges and opportunities of our lives. What are you waiting to do someday that your heart longs to do today? Why wait?

Why not start living the life you've always dreamed of now? Many of us have been groomed through education and culture to think that the best things in life are in the future and that the present is a time of preparation for someday—when I graduate, when I land that perfect job, when I have the money or when I retire. We aren't discounting the importance of preparation—but it's worth considering whether you have brushed aside the deeper dreams that God has placed in you for "someday." Perhaps our impulse to consume comes from continually saying no to the Spirit's call to more abundant living. What can you do now to lean into the good dreams that God has put inside of you, even if it's just one small step?

In the last year that Scott worked as a real estate broker he made almost $500,000. He also spent almost every dime on motorcycles, luxury vacations, the mortgage on a hillside home and a six-digit tax bill. For Scott, this fast-paced lifestyle was self-destructive and left him feeling empty and unsatisfied. Scott and his wife, JoJo, decided that it was time for a dramatic change. He shut down his real estate business and they rented out their home. They then spent the next eight months working in Bangladesh with the Mennonite Central Committee, helping local women establish cottage businesses to support their families. They returned to Portland with a new vision for their lives. They purchased a modest house, turned their front yard into a vegetable garden and started raising chickens. They also invited others into their new life by renting out the bottom floor of their house to friends, whom they share weekly meals and daily prayer with. Scott decided to put his business skills to work, not to feed his own consumption but to create jobs for others and invest in his community. He bought a pizza cart business downtown and started a coffee shop in their neighborhood as a community gathering space. Scott provides jobs to eight other people, and now that the businesses are up and running he has turned his attention to starting a nonprofit vocational training center. They now live on less than 10 percent of what Scott used to make, but life feels more meaningful and whole.

Does the possibility of a radical shift excite or scare you? Why?

What longing to do good have you been putting on hold by telling yourself "someday"?

What does your heart long to be and do? What would you choose to do today if you let your deeper passions lead you?

What is the craziest thing you can imagine doing that would free up your time and your life to do what you are most passionate about?

TIME BUDGET						
	Current Estimate		Increase or Decrease	Time Budget		
CATEGORY	Hrs/Day	Hrs/Week		Hrs/Day	Hrs/Week	Days/Year
BODY CARE						
Sleep						
Exercise						
One-year goal						
RELATIONSHIPS						
Family						
Friends						
Community						
One-year goal						
WORK OF YOUR HANDS						
Paid work						
Household chores						
Unpaid service						
One-year goal						
SOUL CARE						
Meditation and prayer						
Sabbath keeping						
One-year goal						
REST AND PLAY						
Rest						
Recreation						
Vacation						
One-year goal						
MARGIN						
TOTAL						

Figure 2.1. Time budget

DAILY/WEEKLY RHYTHM							
Time	Sunday	Monday	Tuesday	Wednesday	Thursday	Friday	Saturday
12:00 am							
1:00 am							
2:00 am							
3:00 am							
4:00 am							
5:00 am							
5:30 am							
6:00 am							
6:30 am							
7:00 am							
7:30 am							
8:00 am							
8:30 am							
9:00 am							
9:30 am							
10:00 am							
10:30 am							
11:00 am							
11:30 am							
12:00 pm							
12:30 pm							

Figure 2.2. Daily/weekly rhythm

DAILY/WEEKLY RHYTHM							
Time	**Sunday**	**Monday**	**Tuesday**	**Wednesday**	**Thursday**	**Friday**	**Saturday**
1:00 pm							
1:30 pm							
2:00 pm							
2:30 pm							
3:00 pm							
3:30 pm							
4:00 pm							
4:30 pm							
5:00 pm							
5:30 pm							
6:00 pm							
6:30 pm							
7:00 pm							
7:30 pm							
8:00 pm							
8:30 pm							
9:00 pm							
9:30 pm							
10:00 pm							
10:30 pm							
11:00 pm							
11:30 pm							

Figure 2.2. Daily/weekly rhythm

YEARLY RHYTHMS		
January	February	March
April	May	June
July	August	September
October	November	December

Figure 2.3. Yearly rhythms

My Time Bandits	My Strategy for Creating Boundaries

Figure 2.4. My time bandits

3

Practice Gratitude and Trust

Your kingdom is an everlasting kingdom,
and your dominion endures through all generations.
The LORD is trustworthy in all he promises
and faithful in all he does.
The LORD upholds all who fall
and lifts up all who are bowed down.
The eyes of all look to you,
and you give them their food at the proper time.
You open your hand
and satisfy the desires of every living thing.

PSALM 145:13-16

*G*ratitude flows from a sense of wonder and a bit of magic. Sweet flour covers the ground like dew. Tasty quail settle on a desert plain. You go fishing and find two coins in the mouth of a fish, enough to cover you and your friend's yearly taxes. If these sound too fantastic, how about this: A seed falls into the dirt and over weeks and months, through sunshine and rain, grows into a carrot or a potato that you put into a tasty pot of stew. Every day is full of little miracles—the many ways our Creator cares for and provides for us.

We are inviting you to consider this proposition: you are well cared for by a loving Creator who provides you with everything you need. Do we live in a world of scarcity or abundance? Perhaps you've thought, Well, I can agree that I'm being provided for, but what about everyone who is starving because of famine or war? We'll address those important questions later. For now, let's talk about you. What evidence is there that you are being cared for and that everything you need is being provided?

When you woke up this morning, chances are you slept on a comfortable bed. There was breakfast to eat and perhaps a glass of juice or a good cup of coffee or tea to sip. You put clean clothes on. Odds are that you are reasonably safe and that two more meals and a few snacks are still ahead of you today. For most of us, this is the way it has been nearly every day of our lives. We see evidence of the Creator's care and provision all around us. We hear the birds singing in the morning. The sun rises, rain falls to water the earth, and year after year plants grow that provide oxygen and food for our bodies—and not just calories but tasty morsels that excite the palate. We are not only provided for but lavished with good gifts to enjoy: companionship, meaningful work, music, the beauty of nature and cultures, the good sensations of movement— walking, running, swimming, dancing, creativity, the joy of sexuality and a sense of destiny and yearning for the divine mystery. Life itself, every day, is a gift that ancient voices described as the breath of God (Genesis 2:7). There is something enchanting, sacred and deeply good about being alive, if we'll only pause to breathe, look and see. We embrace the abundance of life by learning to practice gratitude and trust.

EMBRACING A LIFE OF ABUNDANCE

Lisa's early life taught her to live with an abiding sense of abundance, gratitude and trust. She tells the story here in her own words.

I was born in the 1970s but raised in the 1930s. I mean that in the best possible way, of course. I am a farm girl. My mother grew up on a farm. My father grew up on a farm. So did all of my grandparents. I am the sixth child in a family of nine children, and my farm childhood has had a lasting impact on my view of abundance.

Though my family was large and there wasn't much money, I never got the impression that we were poor. My mother tended a garden that was large enough to freeze and can produce to last us all winter. In fact, I never ate vegetables from a store until I was grown and had my own home. There was fresh food all summer— corn, green beans, tomatoes, melons, zucchini, potatoes, raspberries, strawberries, apples, carrots, lettuce, peas, rhubarb, onions and more. In the late summer and fall, we put food away—canning, freezing and storing it in the cold room. Some years we raised chickens and had fresh eggs, and when the hens got too old, they also became part of our food source. We occasionally butchered a pig or traded with a cousin for part of a cow and put the meats in the freezer. In the winter my mom would spend time sewing clothes and quilts. There was always an abundance of food. I remember favorite foods Mom would cook when Dad wasn't home for a meal—rice with raisins cooked in milk, sprinkled with sugar and cinnamon or biscuit dumplings simmered in raisins and applesauce—our favorite comfort foods and also inexpensive to make for a large family. In retrospect I can see where my mom economized with our food, with our home-sewn clothes and in many other ways. However, it wasn't a topic of conversation. My mother worked hard, but did not complain about money. Looking back I now know that the farming crisis of the 1980s proved a difficult time for my family financially, but I didn't really know it then. We had enough and that was good.

I learned from the strong women in my family the power of "can do." There was an abiding assumption that if something could be made, fixed or constructed, we could probably figure out how to do it ourselves. Why not? We were dependent on each other, but not so dependent on outside resources. I would watch my grandparents help Mom build something for the house, butcher the hens or make laundry soap. This has been tremendously empowering to me as an adult. I feel as though I have infinite choices concerning whether I create or consume. I can make my own clothes or buy them at a store or thrift shop. I can make my own food. I could even grow it. We can fix things ourselves or give the job to someone more skilled. I feel free to choose either way and know that it is a choice. Helping one another and making things ourselves taught me that meeting our needs didn't necessarily involve much money, though it would require work. Our security came from being part of an extended family and community.

From my father, I learned trust and generosity. He taught me that money is a tool that we can use for good. I can't count all the ways he gave to our family, my friends and families we knew who were in need. He was not afraid of giving too much or of running out, though he never had much himself. He demonstrated that generosity begets gratefulness and a sense of abundance. He and my mom gave sacrificially—sharing meals with men recently released from prison, providing a home to over one hundred foster kids and welcoming their parents into our lives as well. They believed that there was always enough to share, whether their time, money or possessions. Dad also encouraged me to do what I felt called to do and assured me that if I was doing what I was meant to do, I would have what I need.

I am profoundly grateful for this beginning view of money as a launching place for life. As I entered adulthood and Mark and I got married, a few more things became important to me. We felt called to a life that would probably not be conventional in its income stream, though we weren't sure exactly how that would look. We valued working together and shared a dream of working to help people discover life in the way of Jesus. We wanted to avoid debt so we could be free to pursue the life that we felt called to. We also wanted to be able to stay at home with our kids while they were small.

So, we've lived on one income so we could have the flexibility of time to pursue what matters most to us. It has involved making choices, sometimes difficult choices, between time and money. I've had to take more time in order to save money—cooking more from scratch, buying less, making more, creating our own entertainment rather than paying for it. Sometimes I have struggled, feeling like I'd like to be able to offer more experiences for our kids and felt limited in our ability to pay for those things. However, I am realizing now that they have had rich experiences. They've met lots of interesting people because of where we live and our work. They've been able to live in a city where they have participated in interesting activities and projects. They've been able to pursue their interests. They've been taken care of and have not missed out because of having less money than some of their peers. In fact, you could say they are privileged.

I am aware that our family, along with most of us, are in the top 1 percent in terms of global financial wealth. Living in God's abundance requires me to chew on that. It is easy to accumulate too many things. Our stuff almost breeds in our closets. Meanwhile others don't have enough. I still don't know what to do with that. So, I am trying to move in small ways that seem more just to me. I am trying to spend in ways that do good. I am trying to learn to consume less. I have a deep belief that I can trust God for our needs. That there is plenty—enough so that I can ask, share and trust for what is good.

Perhaps the best thing I've received is an abiding sense of gratitude. It may seem paradoxical, but I've found that as we've lived with less I am more content and grateful for what we do have. I am grateful for the choices I have. I am grateful for the

Common Messages About Wealth and Well-being:

- *We don't have enough.*
- *Most people are more well-off than we are.*
- *We work so hard and deserve some comforts and rewards for our sacrifices.*
- *Wealth equals success.*
- *Rich people are greedy.*
- *Poor people are lazy.*
- *We survived the depression/recession, but only by tightening our belts and storing away extra for a rainy day.*

Not all the messages we get in our families are negative.
How about these?

- *We are blessed and thankful.*
- *Money is a tool for generosity.*
- *Take care of what you have and it will last you a good, long time.*
- *We use what we've been given to celebrate, make friends and create community.*
- *Our resources allow us to make memories and build deeper relationships.*

What are the messages you want to pass on to the next generation?

- *We have enough.*
- *You can make wise choices.*
- *Avoid unnecessary debt.*
- *Enjoy what you have before acquiring more.*
- *You can make, fix or repair many things.*
- *We use our resources justly to help bring about a better world.*
- *Live to work, don't work to live.*

small things. I am grateful for enough. I am learning that more does not equal happier, easier or better. I am content. I am grateful for all the surprises that have come my way—tremendous opportunities for my family, generous friends, work that involves travel, lots of interesting people to know and have in our home. I am deeply grateful for the relationships within our family and with our friends as well. Life is abundant and that abundance is not dependent on money.

EXERCISE: APPRECIATE YOUR ASSETS OF ABUNDANCE

Life can seem scarce rather than abundant when we hurry or forget to savor all that we've been given. Our wealth is not only individual but encompasses the entire economic system we benefit from, including access to goods and services, education, opportunities and the public aid that come with living in a stable postindustrial economy. The poorest person in your city may be better off materially than the average person in another country. Keeping an awareness of global economics in mind, take a few moments to consider and rate the provision you've been given in the following categories, considering whether you have reason to feel satisfied.

Food:	Lacking	Adequate	Luxurious	Satisfaction: Yes/No
Clothing:	Lacking	Adequate	Luxurious	Satisfaction: Yes/No
Shelter/safety:	Lacking	Adequate	Luxurious	Satisfaction: Yes/No
Relationships:	Lacking	Adequate	Luxurious	Satisfaction: Yes/No
Health care:	Lacking	Adequate	Luxurious	Satisfaction: Yes/No
Transportation:	Lacking	Adequate	Luxurious	Satisfaction: Yes/No
Education:	Lacking	Adequate	Luxurious	Satisfaction: Yes/No
Recreation/leisure:	Lacking	Adequate	Luxurious	Satisfaction: Yes/No

In terms of our global context, how well are your needs being met?
Are you generally satisfied with what you have?

What if we measured wealth in purposeful work, simple pleasures and meaningful relationships? Many of the things we enjoy most in life are hard to put a monetary value on. Rate the following assets of abundance in terms of the pleasure and value they bring to you.

	Low Value ——————— High Value				
The beauty of the natural world	1	2	3	4	5
The pleasure of food	1	2	3	4	5
Physical health and safety	1	2	3	4	5
A sense of security and peace	1	2	3	4	5
Physical activity	1	2	3	4	5
Friends and family	1	2	3	4	5
Spiritual awareness	1	2	3	4	5
Romance and sexual intimacy	1	2	3	4	5
Emotional health and support	1	2	3	4	5
Access to information and learning	1	2	3	4	5
Noble and purposeful work	1	2	3	4	5
Realized talents and skills	1	2	3	4	5
Opportunities to love and serve	1	2	3	4	5
Creative expression	1	2	3	4	5
Free time and sabbath rest	1	2	3	4	5
The joy of music	1	2	3	4	5
Access to the arts and culture	1	2	3	4	5
Watching or playing sports	1	2	3	4	5
Character and wisdom	1	2	3	4	5
Patience and joy	1	2	3	4	5
Freedom and liberty	1	2	3	4	5
Strength to endure suffering and loss	1	2	3	4	5
Other _____	1	2	3	4	5

> *Which nonmonetary/nonmaterial assets do you enjoy and appreciate the most?*
>
> *Why do you think we tend to overvalue material possessions and undervalue other assets of abundance?*

What Surprised Me
Hailey Scandrette

I always knew I was being raised a little bit differently than most of my friends, but I grew up in San Francisco, where differences don't matter that much. Growing up in a family with an intentionally simple lifestyle didn't seem that different until I was in my early teens and I started going out with friends.

I was used to shopping at thrift stores and wearing clothes my dad and I had found on the street. And yet I was constantly being asked, "Where on earth did you get that skirt!? It's sooooooo cute!!" I was used to packing a picnic for the day, splitting a $5 burrito or bringing my own snacks to the movies. My friends' parents would often give them $50 whenever we went out. When they wanted to eat at more expensive restaurants, I felt a bit weird when we split the bill; they didn't realize the large chunk it was taking out of my monthly allowance.

Something that surprised me was that my friends whose families had less were almost always more generous. On my sixteenth birthday a friend took me shopping and out to lunch to celebrate. She insisted on treating me, despite the fact that it was her last $25, "because," she said, "you're only going to turn sixteen once!" We shared a $10 meal and she bought me a dress at a thrift store. It wasn't a lavish shopping spree, but I felt so loved.

EXPERIMENT: CELEBRATE YOUR ABUNDANCE

One of the best ways to practice gratitude and trust is to regularly celebrate the abundance you've been given. This week throw a feast for your family or a group of friends. Or, even better, feast with the forgotten by making a special effort to share food with someone who is alone or without a home. Your feast doesn't have to be elaborate or expensive. Prepare a special meal, light some candles, put on some music and celebrate the joy of this moment when you are favored. Take time to savor the meal and tell stories about how good life can be—maybe even get up and dance.

EXPERIMENT: KEEP A DAILY GRATITUDE LOG

The practice of gratitude helps us recognize how we have been lavished and loved. "Give thanks to the LORD, for he is good; his love endures forever" (Psalm 106:1). Living gratefully is an important spiritual discipline because it affirms what is evidentially true—that we are cared for by an abundant Provider who delights to give us many good things. This week keep a daily gratitude log. At the beginning or end of each day write down five things you are thankful for. Try not to repeat. If you write each item in sentence form, your list will begin to take the shape of a poem. For example:

I am grateful for . . .

the taste of coffee in the morning

how sunlight fills a room with warmth

the gentleness of a kiss on the cheek

the power I feel in my legs when I run

Your list could be a random collection of things that move you, or you might pick a theme for each day: food, people, nature. Or you might want to spend some extra time outside looking and listening for signs of God's abundance. At the end of the week read your poetic list to a friend or small group.

A Culture of Gratitude and Trust
Lisa Scandrette

For better or worse, children learn more from observing how we live than from what we say. How can we cultivate gratitude and trust in our kids when we are still learning these things ourselves? Here are a few practices that have been useful in our family.

1. We've tried to be vulnerable with our kids about our own challenges with gratitude and trust. For instance, when I struggle with worry, I share that with my family. Together we discuss what is true (what are the real possibilities?) and how to trust God for the things that are making me anxious. We pray together as a family. When kids see this process modeled, it gives them an avenue for learning to deal with worry.

2. One of my favorite strategies for dealing with worry and cultivating trust is to make a list of things that I am grateful for. One day I was helping our daughter remodel her bedroom and I came across a list. I asked, "What's this?" "Oh, that?" she replied. "That's just a list of things I'm grateful for. I made it when I was having an especially hard time." I hadn't realized that one of my kids had adopted my practice.

3. Many nights at dinner we ask, "What are you grateful for today?" This question prompts me, and I hope our kids, to see where God's gifts have shown up in our lives. It helps us see through a lens of gratitude and abundance and reminds us that we've been cared for.

4. Another common dinnertime question is, "What do you need today?" or "How can we pray for you?" This offers us the chance to remind each other to trust God for our needs and to wait expectantly for what the Maker provides.

CONFRONTING WORRY

Though there is constant and overwhelming evidence that we are cared for and that what we need is being provided, at times we all struggle with worry, fear or anxiety. But we don't all worry about the same things. Some of us tend to worry about personal safety or physical well-being. Will I get sick? What if I get hurt in an accident or crash in a plane? What will I do when I get old? What will happen to me after I die? Some of us worry about money. What if I lose my job? Will I have enough to pay my bills? Some of us worry about our significance. Will I finish my work on time? Am I as successful as I should be? Do people respect me? And some of us worry about our relationships or families. Do my parents approve of my choices? Will my kids turn out all right? Will my partner stay faithful to me? Will my friends keep liking me?

The basic message of the gospel is that God is here, caring for us, and that nothing can happen that will separate us from the eternal love of the Creator. Each of us is a beloved child of God. Perhaps this is why the Scriptures continually say, "Do not be afraid" (John 14:27) and why trust was a hallmark of Jesus' message.

Therefore I tell you, do not worry about your life, what you will eat or drink; or about your body, what you will wear. Is not life more than food, and the body more than clothes? Look at the birds of the air; they do not sow or reap or store away in barns, and yet your heavenly Father feeds them. Are you not much more valuable than they? Can any one of you by worrying add a single hour to your life? (Matthew 6:25-27)

Do you believe you can trust God to provide what you need? What in your experience creates doubts about this? What in your experience confirms that what you need will always be provided?

EXPERIMENT: CONFRONTING WORRY

Using figure 3.1, take steps to confront your worries and fears.

First, make a list of the things you typically worry about. You could brainstorm a list or track what you tend to worry about over the course of a week. We once made this a group activity and set up a shared phone number to text the group each time we found ourselves worrying. We prayed for each other whenever we received a text. When we tried this we were surprised by how often we all worried—especially on Monday morning at the beginning of the work week.

When you look at your list of worries, do you notice any patterns or themes?

Second, as a thought experiment, consider the worst-case scenario for what you worry about. Very rarely are our worst fears realistic or probable, but what if they did come true? Let's say there is a very real possibility that you will lose your job. What's the worst thing that

CONFRONTING WORRY			
Step			
1. Name the worry			
2. Worst case scenario			
3. Disordered attachment			
4. Statement of trust			
5. Counteractive measure			

Figure 3.1. Confronting worry

could happen? You will have to look for a new job or possibly relocate. What if you don't find other work in your field over many months? You may have to take a job that is below your pay expectations or skill level. Perhaps you'll have to sell your house or move out of your apartment and move in with a relative or friend, which in the end, might give you a chance to depend more on others.

Here's a more serious example. Let's say your doctor discovers an abnormality and orders tests to determine whether you have cancer. What's the worst thing that could happen? You have cancer and have to go through treatment. What if the cancer is advanced or inoperable? Your life will likely be shorter than you expected. Many people in this situation actually learn to see their terminal illness as a gift because it helps clarify what's really important and valuable in their final months or years. The worst thing that can happen is that you die prematurely and have an early entrance into the paradise of God. The disordered attachment revealed here is a fear or denial of death. But we are each going to die someday. The hope of the gospel is that even death cannot separate us from the eternal love of our Creator (Romans 8:37-39).

Third, explore possible disordered attachments. What makes us anxious, worried or afraid may reveal what we have a disordered attachment to—meaning that we are placing our confidence in things that were never designed to be a true source of security or identity. Many of our everyday fears and anxieties aren't as serious as the loss of a job or terminal illness, but they can be just as paralyzing. I (Mark) often travel to speak at conferences, universities and churches. When I get off the plane I'm often seized by a sense of anxiety. What if I don't do a good job? What if the audience doesn't think I'm interesting or profound? What's the worst thing that can happen? I don't connect with the audience, don't get invited back and feel like a failure. For me this thought experiment reveals a disordered attachment to being thought of as a good and wise teacher. The reality is that my true significance, value and happiness don't hinge on my success as a teacher. I am valuable simply because of who I am, not because of what I accomplish.

Here's an example from Lisa's experience. Recently, while our daughter was in the process of registering for her university classes, she was informed that there was an issue with the validity of her transcript that might prevent her from being accepted as a student. This put Lisa in a panic, and for several nights it was hard for her to sleep. What's the worst thing that could happen? Our daughter would have to defer enrollment or apply to another school. This wasn't what we expected, but there was no particular reason that Hailey had to go to that school. When Lisa reflected honestly on her anxiety, she realized that behind her worry was the fact that because we educated our daughter at home and Lisa developed the transcript, the possible rejection felt like a critique of her competency as an educator—something that she has invested much of her time and energy toward over the past fifteen years.

What do your worries reveal about potential disordered attachments?

Fourth, turn your worries into statements of trust. For each worry on your list, develop a statement of trust. For instance, "I worry that I will lose my job" can become "I trust that you will give me the work and income that I need." Or "I worry that I won't have enough saved for old age" becomes "I trust that you will care for me as you have in all of my days."

How can you affirm the truth that you are cared for?

A fifth step is developing a counteractive measure. A counteractive measure is an action you take to confront your worry head-on. Sometimes we need to act our way into a new way of thinking. Brainstorm a provocative or symbolic action you might take to confront your pattern of worry or anxiety. Our friend Jeff decided to confront his fear of earthquakes by leaving his emergency kit, which he usually took with him, at home. Our friends Chad and Naomi tended to find their security in their home and bank accounts. To confront this attachment they decided to give away a significant amount of money. But then they realized that even giving away money can be a source of pride and power. So they took three $100 bills and burned them as a symbolic way of saying, "We choose to put our faith in God rather than the value of this currency."

Dave's greatest fear wasn't about money or personal safety. When he tracked his worries for a week, he noticed that he felt anxious every time a doubt surfaced in his mind about whether he was truly special or important. He decided to do an experiment to help himself believe the truth that he couldn't be more loved or affirmed than he already is. He realized that many of his decisions and actions were motivated by a desire to be noticed. To counteract this tendency, he decided to do three secret acts of goodness to serve his family, his faith community and his neighborhood over the course of a week.

What steps could you take to confront the things you tend to worry about?

One morning while he was out walking his dog, he noticed that his neighbor's trash had been knocked over by raccoons. Looking at the piles of wet food garbage strewn about the street, he thought, I should let my neighbor know that his garbage got knocked over. But then he stopped himself and decided that this could be one of his secret acts of service. Just after he'd finished scooping up all the wet trash, another neighbor approached and said, "I want you to know that I'm grateful for what you do . . . to care for your dog!" Dave's dog is partially paralyzed and walks with the aid of a doggy wheelchair. A few minutes later when Dave rounded the corner of his street, another neighbor, whom he hadn't previously met, pulled up in a car, rolled down the window and said, "I just wanted to tell you how proud we all are of you for the way you care so well for your dog!" Dave had no ego about caring for his dog, so it was uncanny that in one morning two people would notice and affirm him after he'd decided to do good in secret. Later Dave reflected, "I got noticed and affirmed, but not for the ways that I wanted to be seen. I think God was trying to tell me something, 'You don't have to be anxious about your identity. You can trust that I see and delight in you.'"

NEGOTIATING TRUST

> The Lord is near. Do not be anxious about anything, but in every situation, by prayer and petition, with thanksgiving, present your requests to God. And the peace of God, which transcends all understanding, will guard your hearts and your minds in Christ Jesus. (Philippians 4:5-7)

We often worry about the unknowns that we have little or no control over. Part of an authentic spiritual journey is learning to be comfortable with the mysteries and uncertainties of life—trusting that our Creator is present and caring, and receiving our lives as they have been given to us. Sometimes trust involves releasing our expectations that life has to be a certain way. If we are honest, we don't really know what will make us truly happy or fulfilled. Perhaps faith is having confidence that someone greater than ourselves is participating in the details of our lives.

What if each of our lives is like an epic story—a story that has interesting and attractive characters (that's us)? In books and film a problem or crisis is introduced and we watch to see how the main characters will rise to the challenge, or we wait for some unexpected or miraculous intervention. Most Hollywood stories follow a predictable pattern and even while we watch the main characters struggle and suffer, we know that it will turn out good for them in the end. Right now we are in the middle of our own stories. We experience our lives subjectively and with some uncertainty about how things will turn out. What can we do when we struggle, suffer or feel danger?

We can remember how God has been faithful to us in the past.

> I remember the days of long ago;
> I meditate on all your works
> and consider what your hands have done. (Psalm 143:5)

We can complain to God about the suffering and struggles of our circumstances. "Hear me, my God, as I voice my complaint; protect my life" (Psalm 64:1). And we can ask for God's help in the way that Jesus prompted his disciples to pray with persistence and expectation. "Ask and it will be given to you; seek and you will find; knock and the door will be opened to you. For everyone who asks receives; the one who seeks finds; and to the one who knocks, the door will be opened" (Matthew 7:7-8).

Hearing these invitations to ask for divine help, some of us may wonder whether God actually intervenes in human affairs or simply allows events to play out as they will. This quandary about God's participation has been wrestled with intellectually throughout the centuries. But another way to address the question of divine intervention is through experimentation—by taking the risk to ask. For much of the time life seemingly follows a predictable flow of cause and effect. But then there are moments of unexpected surprises and impossible reversals of fortune. The cancer goes into remission. The couple who have failed to conceive for fifteen years suddenly discover that they are pregnant. A relationship that seemed irrevocably broken begins to heal and become restored. Perhaps sometimes we should imagine and anticipate the seemingly impossible, asking God to act.

ASK, SEEK AND KNOCK

George Müller (1805-1898) is a well-known historical example of someone who took this teaching of Jesus literally. Throughout his life he privately asked God for the resources needed to build orphanages and fund missionary endeavors around the world. He would often ask for very specific amounts for urgent concerns, without letting anyone else know about the need. He kept scrupulous notes of his requests and subsequent answers to prayer, which are described in detail in his autobiography. It's estimated that over a lifetime, he was able to give away the equivalent of millions of dollars in unsolicited funds that came in response to his prayers. One reason to keep good financial records is that it can help you see more clearly the many ways that you are being provided for.

In our early twenties we decided to experiment with this approach by asking God directly for things we needed. When our first child was about to be born, we needed three dozen cloth diapers, but only had $18. Lisa prayed that she could find the diapers for that price. When she went to the store, she found the exact number of diapers we needed on the sale rack for exactly the amount we had, even though they regularly would have cost $54.

The first four years we were married we ran a project serving at-risk children living in low-income housing projects. Many of their parents struggled with mental illness and chemical dependency. We wanted to provide these kids with opportunities to spend time in nature away from the difficulties of their home life. At the time we owned a small economy car that could transport five people with seat belts. But often many more kids wanted to come along. Sometimes we had to turn kids away, and other times, for short distances, we would cram seven or eight people into our little car. After reflecting on the challenge to "ask, seek and knock" we decided to risk a very specific request. Together we prayed for a van with more seats to transport kids. When we prayed, I imagined a big old rusty gas-guzzling van. At the time our organization was underfunded and we hadn't been paid in two months—so there was no way that we could buy the van ourselves. We hadn't told anyone about our prayer, but one night a few weeks later a stranger called to say that she was impressed with our work and wanted to buy us a van—not an old rusty van but a late-model minivan she had picked out for us at the dealership. The next day we drove the van off the lot and right over to the housing projects, where we picked up a parcel of kids to take to the beach. For us this was a clear sign that God had answered our prayer in a remarkable way that encouraged us to trust.

We think it's possible that God wants to give us not only what we need but sometimes even what we want—because our Creator delights in us. Here's a somewhat silly example. I (Mark) love fashion, especially well-designed footwear. Occasionally I'll go to a boutique to look at shoes like some people might visit an art gallery. I saw a pair of expensive handmade shoes that I just loved. But spending that much on a pair of shoes didn't match our spending plan. As I walked away from the store, I thought about the delight that God has for each of us, so I took a risk. I whispered, "God, I know it's not essential, but sometime I would love to own a pair of shoes like the ones I just saw." A week later I saw those same shoes at a garage sale. They were brand new and in my size and the person sold them to me for $5!

EXPERIMENT: ASK, SEEK, KNOCK

Can we really expect that God will give us what we ask for? Do an experiment to test whether this promise is actually true. Consider asking for three to five things you need or desire. Review the list each day for thirty days and look expectantly for signs of provision or response.

4

Believe You Have Enough

Keep your lives free from the love of money and be content
with what you have, because God has said,
"Never will I leave you;
never will I forsake you."

HEBREWS 13:5

I could not have been more excited when my parents announced that we would be spending our vacation at Disney World. My mind raced with visions of the happiest place on earth, which I'd seen portrayed on the Wonderful World of Disney weekly television show. The night before our visit to the Magic Kingdom I hardly slept. For months I'd dreamed of walking through those gates to be greeted by Mickey Mouse. The moment finally came and it was magical, all the flowers and colors and the animatronic rides based on my favorite storybook characters. But after waiting in long lines in the hot sun for several hours, my initial rush of euphoria quickly wore off. I got hungry, the lines became longer, and gradually the happiest place on earth didn't feel quite so happy anymore. My parents bought me an ice cream cone, and I had some money to spend at the gift shop. But everywhere I looked there were more bright and shiny things to buy: cotton candy, plush stuffed toys, T-shirts and souvenir glasses. Soon instead of relishing my time in the Magic Kingdom, I was preoccupied with wanting more.

When our kids were small we returned to the Magic Kingdom. I saw many children like me, holding balloons with cotton-candy sticky fingers, whining, sulking or crying in the middle of the happiest place on earth. Is this kind of behavior simply the result of a missed nap time, crashing sugar levels, a park intentionally designed to encourage conspicuous spending or something deeper? No matter how much we are lavished, we seem to want more, and that desire breeds unhappiness and discontent.

As a little kid your views on money and wealth often have very little to do with reality. When I was small I wondered if we were rich or poor and it was very hard for me to determine. I didn't notice if my friends had nicer cars or houses than we did, or if they wore more expensive clothing. But I did notice that one of my friends got her own gingerbread house to decorate at Christmastime, and I had to share with my two younger brothers. I assumed that we didn't get to decorate individual gingerbread houses because we couldn't afford them. Therefore we must be poor—which was fine by me. As a lover of fairytales and classic children's literature, being poor seemed to be an advantage. Cinderella was poor. The Little Princess was poor. Most of the characters I admired started out with next to nothing, overcame adversity and then lived happily ever after. I always figured that starting out poor was a pretty good setup for having a great story. So I was quite disappointed later when I discovered that having us share a gingerbread house had nothing to do with money. My mom made the gingerbread house herself and explained that it was hard enough just to get one glued together in time for us to decorate.

This is not a new problem. The wise teacher of Ecclesiastes observed that "the eye never has enough of seeing, / nor the ear its fill of hearing" (Ecclesiastes 1:8). A struggle with contentment seems to be at the heart of the ancient story of lost innocence. Adam and Eve were living in what appears to be a garden paradise, filled with abundance and all that is good, including the presence of God. All it took for them to lose the joy of living in this magic kingdom was the suggestion that more would make them happier. The serpent merely suggested that they were being deprived of something better, which God was withholding: "For God knows that when you eat from [the tree] your eyes will be opened, and you will be like God" (Genesis 3:5). The lie of scarcity became their defining perception of reality, unleashing misery and pain that continues to plague humanity. When we see the world through eyes of scarcity and greed, it robs us of the joy in the good lives we have received.

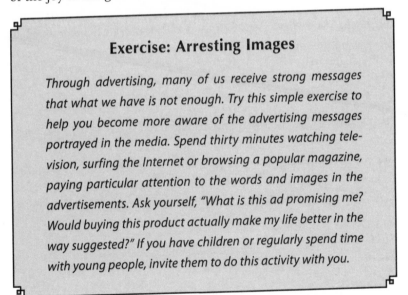

Exercise: Arresting Images

Through advertising, many of us receive strong messages that what we have is not enough. Try this simple exercise to help you become more aware of the advertising messages portrayed in the media. Spend thirty minutes watching television, surfing the Internet or browsing a popular magazine, paying particular attention to the words and images in the advertisements. Ask yourself, "What is this ad promising me? Would buying this product actually make my life better in the way suggested?" If you have children or regularly spend time with young people, invite them to do this activity with you.

We live in a culture that reflects our collective sense of discontent. Since the 1950s the average size of an American home has nearly tripled, while family size has decreased by 30 percent.[1] From dinner plates to bagels, we seem to like it bigger. Why go for small or medium when you can have the large for only twenty-nine cents more? And the consequences of our insatiable appetites for more are devastating. According to the Centers for Disease Control, due to inactivity and readily available inexpensive and subsidized commodity-based processed foods, over a third of us (36 percent) are clinically obese.[2] Within six months, only 1 percent of everything the average person buys is still in use. The other 99 percent has been discarded and is already on its way to a landfill or other disposal site.[3]

Believing that we don't have "enough" or that we need more to be happy has personal and global consequences. We use up precious natural resources and ask our global neighbors to work slave-wage jobs so that we can have what we want for a few cents less. At the root of desperate poverty, human trafficking, political violence and global inequity is a sense of scarcity and competition fueled by greed—the inordinate desire to possess wealth, goods or objects of abstract value far beyond the dictates of basic survival or comfort.

DOES HAVING MORE MAKE US HAPPIER?

First World visitors to the Two-Thirds World are often shocked by the absence of the luxuries and conveniences they are accustomed to, as well as the lack of infrastructure, clean water, public safety, basic nutrition and health care. Yet most people are equally shocked by how generous and happy so many people living in these conditions are—smiling, laughing, singing, dancing and sharing what little they have with one another. First World visitors often confess

---

[1]See "Right Size House," *Build It Smart,* accessed December 6, 2012, www.builditsmartvc .org/how/how0111.php.

[2]"Overweight and Obesity," Centers for Disease Control and Prevention, accessed December 6, 2012, www.cdc.gov/obesity/data/adult.html.

[3]Annie Leonard, "Story of Stuff," excerpted from David Korten, "Economies for Life," in *YES!* Fall 2002, http://dev.storyofstuff.org/wp-content/uploads/2011/10/annie_leonard_ footnoted_script.pdf.

that people living in deprivation seem happier than we are. While being careful not to romanticize or trivialize the challenges of those living with so much less, it seems clear that human happiness is not wholly dependent on what we own. As Jesus rightly observed, a person's "life does not consist in an abundance of possessions" (Luke 12:15).

Much of our striving and conspicuous consumption comes from the misguided notion that more will make us happy: more possessions, more food, more entertainment, more money. Money is the liquid form of desire that gives us the power to buy what we believe will make us happy. How much money does it take to be happy? A recent study suggests that a person's sense of well-being increases with income, but the quality of daily emotional experience levels off at $75,000 in contemporary US dollars. The authors of this Princeton University report concluded that "beyond $75,000, higher income is neither the road to experienced happiness nor the road to the relief of unhappiness or stress."[4] Though it's easy to envy those who have more, "each heart knows its own bitterness, and no one else can share its joy" (Proverbs 14:10).

During the dot-com boom of the 1990s, we knew a family who started a well-known Internet company. When they sold the company and divided up the profits, several family members received over $100 million. A hundred million dollars may sound like a lot, but our friend told us that once he'd gone to work for the new parent company, he was "the little guy" compared with his new associates, who flew to work in their ten-million-dollar private jets. Now that they had acquired venture capital, the next carrot was to invest in disruptive innovations to multiply their wealth. It was hard for our friend to resist the pressure to acquire and achieve more in this new realm.

No matter how much we have, we can always find someone who

---

[4]Daniel Kahneman and Angus Deaton, "High Income Improves Evaluation of Life but Not Emotional Well-Being," Center for Health and Well-being, Princeton University, August 4, 2010, wws.princeton.edu/news/Income_Happiness/Happiness_Money_Report.pdf.

has more. While this may be an extreme example, most of us can relate to the subtle desire for more—better food and clothes, a nicer car, a larger home, more exotic travel. Many of our parents have enjoyed a higher standard of living than our grandparents did. Often the unwritten expectation is that each generation will acquire and achieve more than the previous. Of course this makes sense for families who immigrated to a new country for freedom and a better life. But how much is enough?

EMBRACING VOLUNTARY LIMITS

Our postindustrial economy has brought about unprecedented opportunities for humans to generate disposable income and wealth. In the agrarian economy of the past, the creation of wealth was largely limited by what the land could produce in a given year. Most people had what they needed, with little extra. But with the dawn of an industrial economy and the emergence of cheaply made mass-produced goods, suddenly the average person could expect to have money left over to buy nonessentials. In our time, due to incomes that far exceed the amount needed for basic necessities, along with easy consumer credit, we have the ability to purchase more than we actually need or can realistically use or enjoy. For example, the relative cost of clothing has decreased dramatically over the past one hundred years.[5] Yet instead of limiting our clothing purchases, most of us now simply have far more clothes in our closets than we can possibly wear. Sometimes we make ourselves feel better by donating these clothes to charity. But quite often, no one needs the twenty-seven cheaply made and out-of-date shirts from our closets. And shipping these used items overseas has in many instances devastated a local thriving garment industry.[6] To pursue contentment we

---

[5]See Elizabeth L. Cline, *Overdressed: The Shockingly High Cost of Cheap Fashion* (New York: Portfolio, 2012).

[6]Andrew Brooks, "Stretching Global Production Networks: The International Second-Hand Clothing Trade," Academia.edu, 2012, www.academia.edu/1517438/Stretching_Global_

may need to learn how to buy less and perhaps pay more for food and clothing that is produced and manufactured locally, ethically and sustainably.

We often buy things for emotional reasons. Studies suggest that dopamine is released when we shop.[7] Many of us go shopping as a form of "retail therapy" to manage stress or seek comfort. As one woman told us, "I go to the mall on Friday nights hoping to relax by shopping. But within five minutes of setting the bags down at home, I often feel empty again. And now I have to find space to shove more stuff into my drawers and closets." Buying and consuming can easily become a disordered attachment, a way we seek deeper fulfillment in something that was never designed for that purpose.

Duane Elgin, among others, has suggested that we face a problem most previous generations never had to deal with—learning to say no or enough to our consumer impulses. For a majority of people in previous generations external factors placed limits on consumption.[8] Living in a time when most of us have the ability to buy more than we need requires new skills and provides us with the opportunity, and perhaps the responsibility, to choose voluntary limits to our consumption.

LESS IS MORE

Every few years we receive a visit from our friend Evan Howard, a small man with a quick smile who, sporting a beret and handmade woolen clothes, looks like a goatherder or a medieval philosopher. He is, in fact, both a philosopher and a goatherder. Evan and his wife, Cheri, live on thirty-five acres in the high desert of Colorado, where they raised their two daughters and have lived a self-styled

---

Production_Networks_The_International_Second-hand_Clothing_Trade.

[7]Dan Tynan, "Shopping IS Good for You: How Manolos Can Save Your Life," *Women's Health*, December 2008, www.womenshealthmag.com/life/benefits-of-shopping.

[8]See Duane Elgin, *Voluntary Simplicity*, 2nd ed. (New York: Harper, 2010).

life of voluntary simplicity for the past sixteen years. For Evan this means devoting his time to a rhythm of prayer, manual labor, study, teaching and providing spiritual direction. For the past thirty-two years they have grown or raised some of their own food and lived on $10,000-12,000 per year. They bought their mobile home trailer for $5,000, which they have improved, adding a guest house and additional rooms using salvaged materials. For most of the time we've known Evan, the only way to contact him has been through written correspondence. Recently, though, he has obtained an email address and cell phone, which allowed us to have a conversation about the life he and Cheri have chosen.

So, Evan, what first led the two of you toward a life of voluntary simplicity?

In college we became aware of two issues that triggered our concern: world hunger and the struggle for racial equality and women's rights. This concern came from our study of the Scriptures and was confirmed through books like Ron Sider's *Rich Christians in an Age of Hunger.* We felt called to pursue a lifestyle based on four values: stewardship of resources, justice, nutrition and ecology. For us it started with food. Along with other students at Whitworth University, we chose to be part of an alternative eating plan by making a commitment to eat lower on the food chain while avoiding processed and packaged foods.

How did reading the Scriptures lead you to an awakening about food politics?

Cheri and I had both been taught to read the Bible from an individualistic perspective—viewing its message as mostly about me and my relationship with God. Through studying the book of Amos and other prophetic texts we discovered that the Bible also speaks to structural evil and our responsibilities to one another. The Bible isn't neutral about how we use land or treat people affected by our choices. We came to recognize how our habits of consumption, specifically the food we put in our bodies, are connected to struc-

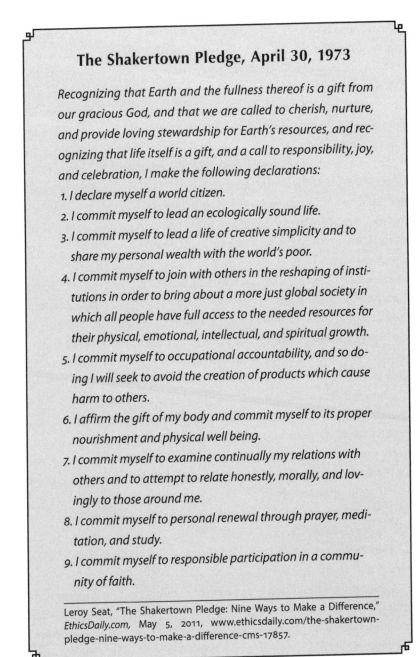

The Shakertown Pledge, April 30, 1973

Recognizing that Earth and the fullness thereof is a gift from our gracious God, and that we are called to cherish, nurture, and provide loving stewardship for Earth's resources, and recognizing that life itself is a gift, and a call to responsibility, joy, and celebration, I make the following declarations:

1. *I declare myself a world citizen.*
2. *I commit myself to lead an ecologically sound life.*
3. *I commit myself to lead a life of creative simplicity and to share my personal wealth with the world's poor.*
4. *I commit myself to join with others in the reshaping of institutions in order to bring about a more just global society in which all people have full access to the needed resources for their physical, emotional, intellectual, and spiritual growth.*
5. *I commit myself to occupational accountability, and so doing I will seek to avoid the creation of products which cause harm to others.*
6. *I affirm the gift of my body and commit myself to its proper nourishment and physical well being.*
7. *I commit myself to examine continually my relations with others and to attempt to relate honestly, morally, and lovingly to those around me.*
8. *I commit myself to personal renewal through prayer, meditation, and study.*
9. *I commit myself to responsible participation in a community of faith.*

Leroy Seat, "The Shakertown Pledge: Nine Ways to Make a Difference," *EthicsDaily.com*, May 5, 2011, www.ethicsdaily.com/the-shakertown-pledge-nine-ways-to-make-a-difference-cms-17857.

tures and systems of injustice. The way we get our food has an impact on other people and the earth itself. If we only give money to help the poor without asking why they are poor or recognizing the systems that support injustice, then we aren't addressing the problem at every level. Adopting a more sustainable lifestyle was a personal step we could take to address structural inequity and ecological destruction.

So, what were some of your first steps toward voluntary simplicity?

In 1978 we signed a document called "The Shakertown Pledge" and made a commitment to live at or below the federal poverty level. We also decided that we wouldn't apply for food stamps or Medicaid even if we qualified. This became a challenging game of sorts. In 1980 we started growing vegetables in our yard, and a few years later began raising chickens. We had read a booklet called *Taking Charge: A Process Packet for Simple Living* that gave really practical steps on how to live more simply. When I was getting my PhD at Berkeley in 1990, we lived in Richmond, California. I worked three days a week and we made $1,200 a month. Our rent was $700 so we had to figure out how to provide for a family of four on the remaining $500.

Our adopted lifestyle gave us so many new options. We found out that if you don't need money, there are all kinds of things to do with your time. Sometimes people ask, "What do you do for fun if you can't afford to go out?" And I usually say, "We live for fun—we get to live the life we've dreamed of." Once a year we might buy tickets to a concert and go out to a nice restaurant, but these are rare and wonderful occasions.

That makes me want to ask, what have been the costs and tradeoffs of the life you've chosen?

I must admit that I don't really enjoy cleaning out our composting toilet, especially in the winter. When the girls were young, we often wondered if we were somehow depriving them. Some of our choices made our parents nervous, and there were minor tensions around gift-giving at birthdays and holidays. One of our daughters recently asked, "Dad, I can't remember, did we ever go to a restaurant? Did we ever buy new clothes at a store?" Choosing this life has meant that our choices are limited. Life is slow. We don't own a microwave. We've been collecting rocks to build the addition onto our house for ten years.

Not having the money to go out and buy what we may need has also forced us to become more resourceful and creative. When something breaks, we work through a decision-making process: Can we fix it? Can we live with it? Do we really need it? Where or how can we get it replaced? Following this method, we've run several cars into the ground and a lot of our stuff is held together with baling wire and duct tape.

As we get older health insurance has become our largest expense, over half of our income, even though we rarely go to the doctor. Probably the toughest cost for me has been missing out on the stimulation of an academic community. Choosing a life of obscurity has limited my teaching and writing opportunities. But I believe the best I can do for humankind comes from this solitude and my vocation as a scholarly contemplative.

Sometimes people who claim to live a radically simple life have "a secret"—they inherited a large sum of money or live somewhere for free. Do you have a hidden source that makes your life possible?

That's funny. We've noticed that as a response to our story, some people try to poke holes—as if we have some special advantages that allow us to live this way. Cheri's college was paid for, and I think we got a $7,000 inheritance that helped us pay off our land. But Cheri is quick to point out that those "advantages" account for a very small portion of our livelihood. I make about $400 a year on book royalties and maybe $2,000 from teaching a class or two at the local community college. Most of our money comes from our work repairing fencing on a ranch owned by Cheri's father. What's allowed us this freedom is our willingness to live at the lowest standard possible in the United States. How many people would be content living in an old trailer home if they had another choice?

How has the way you see simplicity evolved over time?

At first we were motivated by a desire to resist systems of oppression. Then we began to explore the inner aspect and spiritual dimensions of simplicity—things like contentment, humility and making space for contemplation and prayer. Now we resonate with what Wendell Berry would describe as a commitment to the land and the community that is part of a place. Our life is a celebration of the ordinary.

Sometimes people ask me what I'll do when I'm too old to work. Well, I've invested in my family, my neighbors and my church. Those people will take care of me as I've taken care of them. We belong to one another.

EXPERIMENT: DISCIPLINES OF CONTENTMENT

We are challenged to believe that we live in a world of abundance and that our true happiness comes from receiving the lives we've been given. As with all of his teachings, Jesus' instructions about money and wealth point to the heart and invite us into greater freedom. They are designed to help us see accurately that we live in a world where God provides all that we need.

Take a voluntary fast. To experience the freedom of enough requires us to take new risks of action and practice.

For thousands of years the discipline of fasting has helped earnest spiritual seekers to curb the desire for more and to distinguish between needs and wants. Jesus seemed to have assumed that his followers would fast (Matthew 6:16). A fast can also help to reveal our disordered attachments—those things we habitually go to that are not a true or lasting source of comfort. Many people find that abstaining from something they normally use as a coping mechanism brings them face to face with pain, worries or deeper wounds they have been avoiding. Dallas Willard suggests that fasting helps prepare us to do good, because it trains us to say no to bodily desires in favor of intentional choices of obedience.[9]

What do your patterns of spending and consumption reveal about a potential disordered attachment? Is there something that you consume on a daily or regular basis that would be revealing for you to abstain from this week (snacks, coffee, alcohol, media, meat)? As an act of contentment commit to a seven-day fast from something you regularly enjoy. If you choose coffee, for instance, and you usually drink three or four cups a day, your body may go through withdrawal. To avoid headaches, you may want to taper off your consumption over three or four days (e.g., one less cup of coffee each day). Remember, your fast is something between you and God. Jesus taught that fasting should be done discreetly, in a way that wouldn't be obvious to others (Matthew 6:16).

You may also want to consider the potential benefits of a longer-term fast of some kind. Our friend Melanie has challenged herself to live on $1.50 a day for forty days, giving the money she saves on daily living expenses to an organization that helps people get access to food or clean water. The next year she tried to live on $1 a day. Each year our friend Darren gives up something he enjoys and will miss as a reminder that his true happiness isn't dependent on always having more or getting what he wants. One year he might abstain from meat or caffeine; another year he might abstain from watching movies or buying books. Many people have found it helpful to fast from shopping or buying new clothes for a specified time. To make it more fun, people often make these commitments with a group of friends.

---

[9]Dallas Willard, "Spiritual Disciplines, Spiritual Formation and the Restoration of the Soul," *Journal of Psychology and Theology* 26, no. 1 (Spring 1998), www.dwillard.org/articles/artview.asp?artID=57.

My Last Great Idea
Lisa Scandrette

I have a confession to make: I hoard ideas and have an obsession with craft supplies. Some people buy shoes or clothes to get their fix. My temptation is to buy another craft book or supplies for another project.

To be fair, the craft book can be beautiful, creative and inspiring. The new project will probably end up being a gift for someone. Making gifts is a way I give of myself, infusing the project with prayer and care for the recipient. It's meaningful to me in a way that purchasing a gift is not. All good, right?

The problem comes, though, when the project supplies pile so high that I couldn't use them up in a year (or more!), even if making things was my full-time job. For a few years now I've been trying to turn the tide—challenging myself to start with what I have, using more of what I have than new things I bring into the house. It's been helpful to remember that the books, ideas and supplies on my shelves were yesterday's tempting, newest great idea that I just had to have. Have I taken the time to enjoy it?

Rather than another trip to the craft store, why not use one of those fabulously amazing ideas that I already have? When I do this, I find that I have what I need already on my shelves—often some really lovely supplies!

What are your indulgent things? Try enjoying what you already have: read your unread books, wear the clothes and shoes in your closet, use up your craft supplies. Play a game off your shelf with your friends or family. Try cooking from your pantry for a week without going to the store.

CHOOSING VOLUNTARY SIMPLICITY

> I have stilled and quieted my soul;
>> like a weaned child with its mother;
>> like a weaned child I am content. (Psalm 131:2)

The gospel invites us into a posture of radical contentment and deep satisfaction with the lives we've been given. Throughout history wise people have recognized that our sense of satisfaction needn't come from having more or always having what we want. The apostle Paul famously said, "godliness with contentment is great gain. For we brought nothing into the world, and we can take nothing out of it" (1 Timothy 6:6-7). Elsewhere Paul said, "I have learned the secret of being content in any and every situation. Whether well fed . . . or in want" (Philippians 4:12). What is the secret of contentment? Perhaps it is learning to recognize the difference between needs and wants. Needs are what is basic to our survival (food, clothes and shelter). Perhaps wants are the "more" beyond these needs that we mistakenly believe we are entitled to or will make us happy. Paul's expectation was, "If we have food and clothing, we will be content with that" (1 Timothy 6:8). He knew that when we set our expectations based on true needs, we can live with contentment and satisfaction, receiving anything more as a luxury to enjoy with thanks.

TASK: TAKING STEPS TOWARD VOLUNTARY SIMPLICITY

One expression of contentment is adopting voluntary limits to consumption, and there are several reasons for making this choice. One is financial. You may need to curb spending to live within your means. Another is ethical. You may want to consume less to be a better steward of the earth's resources and to spend in ways that benefit the poorest people in the world. Another is your life energy and goals. It takes time to shop for and maintain the things we own. The following is a list of common areas of consumption (food, clothing, housing, transportation, consumer goods and entertainment). Consider whether you might benefit from taking steps toward voluntary limits or more ethical spending in any of these areas.

Food and drink. How much food and drink is enough? Am I consuming more or less food and drink than my body needs? Or am I consuming just the right amount? (Circle one.)

More   Less   Just Right

What are the personal costs of consuming more or less than I need? Examples: health consequences from an eating disorder or extra weight, excessive food spending, alcohol dependency.

_____

_____

_____

How are other people affected by my choices? What are the global sustainability and environmental costs when I'm not content in this area? Examples: farmland in developing countries used to produce luxury products for foreign markets instead of needed food, fossil fuel depletion to transport goods over thousands of miles.

_____

_____

_____

Is this an area of life where I may actually benefit from having less?

☐ Yes   ☐ No

What might it look like for me to practice contentment and voluntary simplicity with food?

☐ learn to eat regular nutritious meals in the amount my body needs

☐ only eat one serving of food at meal times

☐ cook at home _____ times a week

☐ limit my consumption of meat-based protein to _____ times a week

☐ set a limit to the number of "treats" (e.g., specialty beverages, desserts, etc.) I have to _____ per week

☐ only eat food items that are fair trade and slavery free (especially coffee, tea and chocolate)

☐ other _____

Eating, Emotions and Ethics
Lisa Scandrette

Though we've tried to live simply for many years, I have tended to eat far more food than my body needs to be healthy. Eating has been a way to cope with stress and negative emotions. In the last couple of years, however, I have become increasingly uncomfortable with the thought that while others struggle to have enough, I am eating far more than I need. This has inspired me to learn to handle my food consumption in new, more moderate ways. To do that, I am learning new ways to deal with emotions and stress. I am eating less, eating healthier and reminding myself that I am on a road to a new kind of lifestyle. For me, it is a long, sometimes difficult road where I need to remember that I only need to take one more step right now to becoming a healthier, less greedy consumer of food. As a benefit, I am feeling better physically and living more consistently within my values.

Clothing. How many clothes are enough? Do I have more or less clothes than I need?

More   Less   Just Right

What are the personal costs when I'm not content in this area? Examples: overflowing closets, excessive time spent shopping.

_____

_____

_____

How are other people affected by my choices? What are the global sustainability and environmental costs when I'm not content in this area? Examples: supporting slave-like conditions for workers by acquiring cheaply made clothes.

_____

Is this an area of life where I may actually benefit from having less?

☐ Yes   ☐ No

Guilt-Free
Hailey Scandrette

My parent's attitude toward time and money always made sense to me as a kid, but in the past few years I've had to start considering my personal attitude about these commodities. For instance, over the course of my teen years I converted many of my friends to the ways of thrift shopping and street hunting. In my early teens this was mainly because thrift shopping was cheaper and the clothing was more unique, and I was more likely to find what I wanted at a thrift store. I loved the look on my friend's face when I'd tell her that my cute new sweater was a street find, and when possible I'd pass along my finds to her. Recently I've begun to realize that my love for thrift shopping doesn't come solely from its convenience; it has extensive ethical benefits as well, which I believe are equally (if not more) important than the fact that I'm saving money. Buying (or finding) used clothes is good for the environment, as most textile waste ends up in landfills. It's good for local thrift shops and small businesses, and it doesn't support the unfair wages and life-threatening conditions often associated with the garment industry. In these ways a simple practice like primarily buying used clothing saves me money and is congruent with my ethical values and beliefs—*and* means I get to buy one-of-a-kind vintage dresses 100 percent guilt-free.

What might it look like for me to practice contentment and voluntary simplicity with clothing?

- ☐ commit to only buying used clothes for one year
- ☐ abstain from buying clothes at all for one year
- ☐ limit my wardrobe to a certain number of items and sell or give away the rest
- ☐ commit to only buying ethically made clothing
- ☐ other _____

Housing. How much space do I need? Do I have more or less space than I need?

More   Less   Just Right

What are the personal costs when I'm not content in this area? Examples: sustaining a large mortgage and higher utility costs, time required for maintenance and upkeep.

_____

_____

_____

How are other people affected by my choices? What are the global sustainability and environmental costs when I'm not content in this area? Examples: nonrenewable energy depletion for utilities, construction materials and possibly increased commute time.

_____

_____

_____

Is this an area of life where I may actually benefit from having less?

☐ Yes   ☐ No

What might it look like for me to practice contentment and voluntary simplicity with housing?

- ☐ stay in the apartment or home I have
- ☐ downsize to a smaller space
- ☐ invite someone else to share living space
- ☐ use my space to regularly practice hospitality
- ☐ decrease my heating and cooling use and costs

☐ other_____

Transportation. How much car and airline travel do I need? Do I travel more or less than I need?

More   Less   Just Right

What are the personal costs when I'm not content in this area? Examples: long travel time, less time for exercise, rest and relationships.

_____

_____

_____

How are other people affected by my choices? What are the global sustainability and environmental costs when I'm not content in this area? Examples: dependence on foreign oil and depletion of nonrenewable natural resources, air pollution.

_____

_____

_____

Is this an area of life where I may actually benefit from having less?

☐ Yes   ☐ No

What might it look like for me to practice contentment and voluntary simplicity with my transportation?

☐ limit the number of non-work-related miles I drive per month to _____
☐ take public transportation or carpool to work
☐ walk, bike or take public transportation for local errands and consolidate trips
☐ downsize the number of cars in our household
☐ replace existing vehicle with one that is more energy efficient
☐ limit and consolidate airline travel
☐ purchase carbon credits to neutralize carbon footprint for air travel
☐ other_____

Consumer goods. How much stuff (books, electronics, furniture, cars, bicycles, etc.) do I need? Do I have more or less stuff than I need?

More   Less   Just Right

What are the personal costs when I'm not content in this area? Examples: clutter, overspending, time spent shopping and maintaining possessions.

_____

_____

_____

How are other people affected by my choices? What are the global sustainability and environmental costs when I'm not content in this area? Examples: waste, crowding of landfills, support of cheaply made disposable goods.

_____

_____

_____

Is this an area of life where I may actually benefit from having less?

☐ Yes   ☐ No

What might it look like for me to practice contentment and voluntary simplicity with consumer goods?
- ☐ sell or give away items that I don't need or use regularly
- ☐ extend the life of the items I own, even when they become slightly outdated
- ☐ commit to buying only used items for one year
- ☐ fast from buying new household goods for one year
- ☐ other_____

Entertainment. How much entertainment do I need? Do I have more or less entertainment than I need?

More   Less   Just Right

What are the personal costs when I'm not content in this area? Examples: overspending, disordered focus, avoidance of important tasks or relationships.

_____

_____

_____

How are other people affected by my choices? What are the global sustainability and environmental costs when I'm not content in this area? Examples: unintentional support of unethical messages or industries (adult media, violence, stereotyping).

_____

_____

_____

Is this an area of life where I may actually benefit from having less?

☐ Yes   ☐ No

What might it look like for me to practice contentment and voluntary simplicity with my entertainment? Note: Sometimes entertainment consumption is more an issue of time than money.

☐ limit the number of times a month I eat out per month to _____

☐ limit the amount of money I spend on entertainment to $ _____ per month

☐ limit the time I spend consuming media to _____ hours per week

☐ other _____

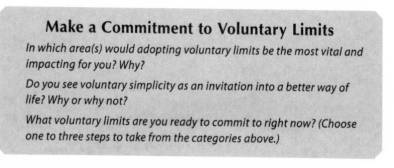

Make a Commitment to Voluntary Limits

In which area(s) would adopting voluntary limits be the most vital and impacting for you? Why?

Do you see voluntary simplicity as an invitation into a better way of life? Why or why not?

What voluntary limits are you ready to commit to right now? (Choose one to three steps to take from the categories above.)

EXPERIMENT: RISK GENEROSITY

In chapter two we told a fantastic story about praying for a van and being given one right off the dealer's lot. Well, there's more to the story. We already had a small car that we'd recently purchased. We didn't need a second car, so our initial thought was to sell our small car and put the money into savings. A few days after receiving the van we drove out to see some friends who were serving a rural church. We took them for a ride across the countryside, and with us they celebrated our blessing and good fortune. After dinner they told us that they were also praying for a new vehicle, since they'd just found out from their mechanic that their car was on its last leg. As we drove home, Lisa turned to me casually and said, "I think we should give Chuck and Karen our old car."

I bristled at the thought and told Lisa that it didn't seem prudent to just give away a vehicle we'd recently paid thousands of dollars for.

"But Mark," she said, "we were just given a vehicle worth so much more. Don't you think we could show our gratitude by sharing what we have with someone else?"

While we were camping over the weekend, we continued to argue about what to do with the car. My anger and sulking really soured the trip. Deep down I knew that Lisa was right. If others had asked me what they should do in the situation, I would have told them it was obvious. When we are blessed, we should bless others. But for some reason I just couldn't let it go. This was our chance to finally have more. I was reminded of a story Jesus once told:

> "Watch out! Be on your guard against all kinds of greed; life does not consist in an abundance of possessions." And he told them this parable: "The ground of a certain rich man yielded an abundant harvest. He thought to himself, 'What shall I do? I have no place to store my crops.' Then he said, 'This is what I'll do. I will tear down my barns and build bigger ones, and there I will store my surplus grain. And I'll say to myself, "You have

plenty of grain laid up for many years. Take life easy; eat, drink and be merry.'"

"But God said to him, 'You fool! This very night your life will be demanded from you. Then who will get what you have prepared for yourself?' This is how it will be with whoever stores up things for themselves but is not rich toward God." (Luke 12:15-21)

These stories are always fun to read, until they speak to your present situation. I was the guy in the story—being greedy with the abundance that I'd been given. Eventually I cooperated with Lisa's generous heart. I knew that I wouldn't feel peace until we'd given the car away to our friends. And when we did, we were the answer to their prayers.

Let's return to an issue brought up in chapter three. I know that I'm cared for and provided for, but what about the millions of people across the world who don't have access to basic nutrition, clean water, safety and health care? Is there really enough for everyone?

Maybe there would be enough if those of us with more choose to be generous. The gospel invites those of us who have enough to spend ourselves on behalf of those who do not (1 Timothy 6:17-19). In the accounts of the ministry of Jesus, generosity was often a sign of belief and repentance. When Zacchaeus, a wealthy tax collector, encountered the unconditional welcome of Jesus, he was prompted to give away half of his possessions and pay back all those he had cheated. In response Jesus said, "Today salvation has come to this house" (see Luke 19:1-10). Jesus told his disciples, "Sell your possessions and give to the poor" (Luke 12:33). And later we see them doing just that (Acts 2:45). The invitation to be so openhanded was a call to believe and act on the reality that we live in a world of abundance rather than scarcity—a world where we can give away what we have and still find that we have enough. Generosity is a sign of contentment and trust in the reality of our Maker's abundance.

> *Why do you think Jesus would tell his disciples, "Sell your possessions and give to the poor"? What did this instruction say about his understanding of how life works?*
>
> *Is this instruction taken seriously by disciples of Jesus today? Why or why not? What would happen if it was?*

EXPERIMENT: HAVE TWO, GIVE ONE

Sometimes a more provocative experiment can shift our lives and thinking in a way that more modest or incremental steps never can. Would you consider selling or giving away half of what you own? Since ancient times truth seekers have divested of their possessions in order to go on a deeper search for meaning and union with God. Why? Perhaps because what we own, to some extent, owns us. Our stuff takes time and attention to maintain and occupies a place in our hearts.

A few years ago, we and a group of our friends tried to see how far we were willing to go to live out radical generosity. Inspired by the words of John the Baptist, "Anyone who has two shirts should share with the one who has none, and anyone who has food should do the same" (Luke 3:11), we decided to sell or give away half of our material possessions, donating the proceeds to global poverty relief. Our goal wasn't to be exacting or legalistic, but to playfully engage each other to live more freely and generously. Each week over eight weeks we would choose a category of possessions to sell, share or give away. One week it would be clothes, another week books and music, and another week, valuables and larger household items like cars and bicycles. As we sorted through our stuff, we often found an item that someone else in the group needed. We sold some items online, others at local resale shops, hosted a garage sale and donated the leftovers to a charity thrift store. It was shocking to find out how little some of our possessions were worth and disappointing that we'd regarded them as so precious. In the end we collected thousands of dollars and sent a check off to a global relief organization.

We realized things about contentment that we never would have learned just by discussion. This experiment caused some of us to permanently change our buying and consumer habits. And we decided that it would be helpful to declutter, sell, share and give away stuff once a year.

Consider doing this experiment with a friend or group of friends. Over the next four weeks, go through your homes and make an inventory of what you own and discern what you are being invited to sell or give way over the next month. You can use the money you generate to (1) help people who are struggling with basic survival and health needs locally and globally, or (2) pay down your personal consumer debt. Here are some ideas on what to do with your stuff:

Sell. Some items can be sold online or at a resale shop, and the rest at a garage sale. Though it may seem tedious to try to sell some items, the process may help you see how you have overvalued your material possessions. Our friend Damon prized his large collection of books. He decided to post each book for sale online, even though on most books he would only make a dollar. The tedious work of wrapping up books and taking them to the post office helped him face his compulsion to continually buy books.

Share. You can cultivate a local economy of interdependence by sharing what you have with people you know. We've learned to ask around before buying items (especially tools or camping equipment) because there is a good chance that someone in our community has what someone else needs and will lend or gift it to them.

Give. If you can't sell the item and don't know anyone who needs it, bring it to a thrift shop.

Recycle. Before throwing things in the trash, sending them to the landfill, find out what can be recycled. Many cities have programs for recycling items like batteries, old paint, electronic equipment and even construction materials.

Is this an experiment you would seriously consider doing? Why or why not?

What kind of resistance or questions come up for you as you contemplate this activity?

What do you think is the proper motive for an experiment like this?

With a practice like this, it's helpful to keep in mind why you are doing it. Take a playful approach. It's voluntary and no one will be looking over your shoulder judging whether you've really gotten rid of exactly half your stuff. See how far you are comfortable going, how much you are willing to risk and what you might discover.

5

Create a Spending Plan

Whoever can be trusted with very little can also be trusted with much, and whoever is dishonest with very little will also be dishonest with much. So if you have not been trustworthy in handling worldly wealth, who will trust you with true riches? And if you have not been trustworthy with someone else's property, who will give you property of your own?

LUKE 16:10-12

When Dani first joined our little neighborhood faith community, she thought it was strange that we talked so openly about our personal finances. As a group activity, each year we create and share spending plans with one another. To newcomers like Dani we explain that we do this because how we manage our finances largely determines whether we are free to spend our time and money on what matters most. We want to encourage and support one another in bringing our time and money into alignment with our deeper goals and values. And for many of us the solidarity of group practice gives us the courage to take steps and make new choices that we might not be able to on our own.

Dani felt vulnerable the first time she shared her spending plan in the meeting. When she created her spending plan, she realized that she was overspending on shopping, concerts and eating out, resulting in several thousand dollars in credit card debt. She resolved to pay off her credit card, which she was able to do in a matter of months. The next year when she prepared her spending plan, she noticed that she was spending 25 percent of her earnings eating out. This was a significant amount, and she realized that this unplanned spending didn't fit with her deeper goals and values. Someday she imagined working in a more creative environment or going to graduate school. The next year she decided to budget significantly less for eating out. To accomplish this she committed to packing her lunch for work and learning to cook nutritious food at home, a skill she hadn't acquired growing up. She asked a couple of friends to show her how to shop at the local farmer's market and to teach her to prepare tasty homemade meals.

After taking steps to simplify her spending, Dani realized that she could live on significantly less. At the time, she worked at a job downtown that provided security and good benefits but wasn't particularly fulfilling. Knowing that she could live on a more modest income, the next year Dani decided to make a shift. She left her downtown office job to work with a local nonprofit whose mission she is deeply passionate about. Dani says,

> Incorporating the value of simplicity in my life these last four years has been a subtle and slow process. Gradually I saw that simplicity was not a denial of enjoyment but focusing on what mattered most, and putting my resources behind those priorities. These choices have ultimately led me to becoming way happier and more fulfilled. I didn't even realize how much I'd changed until I compared my values and practices now with when I first moved to the city. For people who are just beginning to connect their money and their spirituality, it might be comforting to know that it's a process and it's possible, even if, like me, you have anxiety about money.

How we manage and spend our money is an expression of what we truly value. Creating and implementing a spending plan is an important tool for making our vision and life goals a reality. It's a skill that can help us align our time and money with what matters most.

LEARNING TO VALUE AND MANAGE FINANCIAL RESOURCES

One of the things I'm most grateful for is what my parents taught me about budgeting and money management. Beginning when I was three, my parents gave me a weekly allowance of thirty cents. Along with my three dimes they gave me some simple guidance about money that my young mind could grasp: ten cents to give, ten cents to save and ten cents to spend. I put one dime in the plate at Sunday school, another dime in my piggy bank at home and I spent my third dime on bubbles, a rubber ball or some candy at the corner store. Often, I was saving for a larger toy, like the magic trick set I bought when I was six. As I got older my allowance gradually increased. When I was eleven and started making a little money on a weekly paper route, my parents told me they would continue to give me an allowance if I would track my spending using an accountant's ledger. Before getting my allowance I had to show my books, the record of how much I made, how much I spent and how much I currently had in cash and in my savings account. I'll admit that I sometimes resented having to keep track of every cent I earned and spent, but it helped me understand the value of my work and trained me to spend consciously and to save for larger purchases.

I also benefited by seeing good day-to-day financial practices modeled by my parents. One night a month my dad would sit down at the table after dinner to pay the bills and "do the books," meaning that he tracked our family budget and spending using an accountant's ledger and later a computer spreadsheet. My parents used an envelope system to manage their cash spending, a method thought to have originated during the great depression of the 1930s.[1] At the beginning of each month my mom

---

[1]"Envelope System," *Wikipedia*, accessed December 7, 2012, http://en.wikipedia.org/wiki/Envelope_system.

It Was Our Responsibility
Hailey Scandrette

When I was about ten my parents put us in charge of our own budgets with categories. Each category got a certain amount of money deposited to it per month: $10 for charitable giving, $10 for allowance, $20 for clothing, $5 for gifts and $5 for things like going out with friends. We were also encouraged to deposit a portion of money we earned into a savings account for college or larger purchases. It was our responsibility to sit down with one of our parents at regular intervals and do our bookkeeping so that we knew where our money was going and how much we had in each category.

Now that I don't receive any allowance and all the money in my bank account is either earned by me or was given to me by my grandparents to help me pay for college textbooks, it is incredibly useful that I already know how to budget my money and track my spending. I've kept most of the same categories, and thanks to my obsessive saving I've been able to pay half my college tuition through babysitting jobs.

would withdraw a predetermined amount from the bank and put the cash into separate envelopes for specific budget categories like groceries, gas, entertainment and clothing. She knew how much we had left to spend by simply looking in the envelopes. Or if she wanted to spend more in one category, she knew to spend less of the money in another envelope. This method also made monthly record keeping easy. Dad also showed me our family's budget, and both of my parents would often reference whether something we wanted fit into our spending plan. Later, when I had a driver's license and a part-time job, my parents had me pay for things like gas and insurance, while they provided me with access to a car. So by the time I was living on my own, I had a pretty good idea about managing my money and how much it cost to live.

We've used a similar strategy for teaching our kids about money. From an early age we invited them to manage a portion of our family spending plan. By early grade school they were managing their own spending money, clothing allowance, entertainment funds and part of our giving budget. They helped decide what causes and organizations we supported as a family and managed the funds used to buy gifts for their friends' birthdays. They also kept a ledger to track earning, spending and savings. As they've become teenagers they've also started managing their own debit cards, checking and savings accounts that are linked to our family accounts.

Any good parent wants to be generous with their kids. But overspending on kids in an attempt to express love isn't the best idea. We've noticed many parents lavishing their kids with expensive gifts, buying them large-ticket items and putting a twenty-dollar bill in their hand every time they walk out the door. Of course we want to be generous with our kids and provide them with the best resources for their development, but we also believe it's our job to guide them toward being responsible with money and knowing the value of work and saving. With larger ticket items that our kids have wanted, we have partnered with them, matching funds that they have earned or saved themselves to make a purchase. Our daughter Hailey saved for the summer theater camp she enjoyed. Our son Noah purchased a computer and professional camera equipment. Our youngest son, Isaiah, refinished the deck on our house in exchange for a plane ticket to see a good friend. We've noticed that our kids value their possessions and experiences more when they contribute to their purchase; it also makes them feel proud. We think it's important, particularly for kids in their later teens, to see that the money they earn isn't just for buying clothes, music, electronics and going to the movies. Part of what they earn through babysitting or another part-time job should go toward charitable giving and saving for college or other upcoming expenses.

What we learned about budgeting and money management prepared us well for adulthood and the freedom to pursue what matters most to us. When Lisa and I got engaged, we began taking steps to merge our financial lives by opening a joint bank account and creating our first shared spending plan about six months before we were married. Our first family spending plan was pretty simple. We made $935 a month after taxes, plus about $85 in business mileage reimbursement. I've kept the budget in a file as a keepsake. Here's what it looked like, scratched in pencil in a notebook:

Charitable Giving	$150
Gifts	$30
Food	$90
Rent	$250
Utilities	$130
Gas & Insurance	$150
Phone	$25
Entertainment	$25
Health Insurance	$100
Allowances	$20
Savings	$50
Total	**$1,020**

Since we were doing an experiment in radical contentment and generosity, there are a few basic budget items conspicuously absent, such as clothing, travel and medications. At the time we were relatively healthy, didn't plan on having kids for a few years and decided that the clothes we already had would last a while. As part of our experiment we also gave away 15-20 percent of our income.

After creating our first shared budget there were some issues to work out between us. While my family had a more methodical and principled approach to money, Lisa's family emphasized spontaneous generosity. To reach a compromise we decided to designate part of our monthly giving for Lisa to spend on hospitality and spontaneous benevolence. After some time we came to a common understanding about how to navigate our finances. Money was something we talked about extensively during our engagement and first year of marriage.

Our budgeting practices have evolved over time. I used to pay our bills and track our expenses using paper ledger sheets and later a computer spreadsheet. Now most of our bills are on automatic payment through our bank, and Lisa tracks our spending using budgeting software.

Here's how our annual budgeting process works. Toward the end of December or shortly after January 1, we have a family meeting (this one with just the two of us) and look at our average spending in each area of our budget, noticing if there are any categories where our spending plan needs adjustment. Some categories, like food and utilities, go up slightly every year due to inflation. We may decide that another area, like transportation, may go down slightly if we anticipate driving less. We also discuss whether there are any new larger expenses on the horizon like braces for the kids or major home repairs.

One of the things we've learned is to set aside money monthly for forecasted expenses. Most of our expenses are monthly bills, but there are a few larger ticket expenses, like car insurance and property taxes, that are only billed once or twice a year. We calculate how much these expenses are per year, divide that number by twelve and factor it into our monthly spending plan. There are also predictable longer-term expenses that we can plan for like car repairs, medical expenses, vehicle replacement and home maintenance. Our monthly budget reflects what we anticipate having to spend in those areas over multiple years, and we save accordingly. When we need a new hot water heater or it's time to replace our car, we don't panic, because the money has already been allocated and saved. If a spending plan doesn't account for these forecasted expenses, it can seem like there's a lot of extra money laying around to spend. But when a big ticket expense arises, you are caught off-guard and end up scrambling to get a second job, empty a retirement account or take out a loan. Planning for these predictable forecasted expenses can give you peace of mind, live with less urgency and help you become more realistic and sustainable with your discretionary spending.

We've noticed that some people take issue with this methodical approach to budgeting, as if forecasting expenses and planning ahead is opposed to trusting God. Preparing for the future is not the same as greedily hoarding wealth. The wise teacher of Proverbs observed the common sense of planning ahead that is evident in the natural world: "Go to the ant. . . . Consider its ways. . . . It stores its provisions in summer and gathers its food at harvest" (Proverbs 6:6-8). Jesus applied this same wisdom of "counting the cost" to building a tower, going to war or becoming a disciple:

> Suppose one of you wants to build a tower. Won't you first sit down and estimate the cost to see if you have enough money to complete it? For if you lay the foundation and are not able to finish it, everyone who sees it will ridicule you, saying, "This person began to build and wasn't able to finish." (Luke 14:28-30)

Like many people, our yearly earning often fluctuates—in our case, especially in the early days, depending on whether the organization we worked for had adequate funding to pay us. To account for this, we prioritized the categories in our spending plan, beginning with the most essential fixed expenses (like charitable giving, taxes, housing and food), followed by flexible or discretionary spending. If we have a lower-income year or unexpected expenses, then some of our lower-priority spending categories don't get funded—or we spend less in those areas until the end of the year when we have a better idea of whether we'll be able to meet our budgeting goals.

WHY CREATE A SPENDING PLAN?

We think of creating a spending plan as a spiritual discipline akin to prayer, study or service. A spending plan helps us

→ have less anxiety about money

→ get a more realistic picture of our true financial situation

→ feel good about our spending

→ live out our deeper values with greater consistency

→ see more clearly how God is providing for us

→ gain greater clarity about what we need to trust God to provide

→ know whether we have the freedom to change jobs or the flexibility to take time off

→ become more empowered to be intentional about and generous with our giving

→ build common understanding with the people we share financial decision making with

Despite all these advantages, we've noticed that many people resist creating a spending plan. Can you identify with any of these?

I don't make enough to have a spending plan. A budget can be a useful tool at any level of income. Shortly after Lisa and I were married, I started getting together with a couple of friends once a week to check in with each other. We met at a local fast food restaurant, where my two friends each bought a big breakfast, juice and coffee. Every week they made fun of me for only buying a cup of coffee (with free refills). In defense I would say, "Spending $5 a week on breakfast is not part of our spending plan." And one of them would say, "Well, my wife and I don't make enough to even have a spending plan." All three of us were newly married, in our early twenties and working our first jobs in a down economy. I knew I was making the same or less than they were and that $5 a week translated into $20 a month or $240 a year, enough to pay for a plane ticket to visit our parents or a weekend anniversary trip to a bed and breakfast. Three years later one of those two friends was close to bankruptcy and the other was living with his in-laws, while Lisa and I paid cash for our first home. If you have any amount of money, you have the opportunity and responsibility to decide what you will do with it. You can either make those decisions impulsively or reflectively—and the results will be dramatically different.

I make enough that I don't have to concern myself with those small details. Some of us have enough wealth or income that our personal spending seems inconsequential in relation to a much larger portfolio. Or we assume that everything is okay as long as we stay below a certain spending rate or there is money in the account. A friend recently admitted that as his wealth has increased over the past few years, so has his spending, primarily on himself. He resists calculating how much he now spends a month on designer suits, fine dining and luxury accommodations and travel. The total would probably be shocking. A spending plan isn't just useful for controlling spending. It's also a reflection of a person's deeper values and priorities.

I am afraid to find out where my finances are at. A spending plan can help you gain a realistic picture of your current financial status. It requires getting a realistic assessment of how much you earn, how much you spend, how much you have in checking and savings, and what your debts are. Some of us avoid creating a spending plan for the same reason we put off going to the doctor—because we are afraid of what we might find out. So we live in a state of denial about our true financial picture. For some that means continuing to spend at an unsustainable rate. Others may simply not spend or give what they could because of a fear that they might not have enough. Creating and living by a spending plan can help you know how much you are able to sustainably spend—so you can feel good about spending or not spending based on the values and goals you've identified.

I am embarrassed about how much I have. A budget can help you become more conscious and intentional about the wealth that has been entrusted to you. When we've surveyed friends, some have said that they resist using a spending plan because it will reveal how well-off they are and they prefer to think of themselves as someone with less privilege and responsibility. Research shows, somewhat counterintuitively, that having more doesn't necessarily translate into more generous giving.[2] In the dynamic start-up economy of the Bay Area where we live, it's not uncommon for tech workers to become overnight millionaires when their company's stock goes public. Some are unprepared for this level of wealth, believing that people with money are greedy or pretentious or that money is inherently evil. They do not want to become like this, so instead of creating an intentional spending plan that emphasizes charitable giving and wise investing, many spend freely, make poor investments choices and lose a significant portion of initial assets. People who are fortunate enough to be entrusted with wealth are also invited to make wise choices so that they can maximize their generosity.

It's a lot of work to set up a budget and track your spending. How successful would any business be that didn't project expenses and track its earning and spending? Your personal finances are at least as important as any business. Managing money is work. The question is, do you want to put the work in earlier or later? If you choose not to create a spending plan, quite often you'll put the work in on the back end—switching money between accounts, dealing with creditors or spending nights and weekends digging through receipts and bank statements during tax season. When you set up a yearly spending plan and a money tracking system, you've put the work in ahead of time. The rest of the year you can simply work the plan without having to worry about whether there will be enough money in the account so the rent or mortgage check doesn't bounce.

> *Do you relate to any of these reasons for resistance to using a spending plan? Explain.*
>
> *What do you think are the benefits of creating and using a spending plan? How have you experienced those benefits personally?*

[2]Emily Gipple and Ben Gose, "America's Generosity Divide," *The Chronicle of Philanthropy*, August 19, 2012, http://philanthropy.com/article/America-s-Generosity-Divide/133775/.

TASK: TAKE STEPS TO CREATE A PERSONAL SPENDING PLAN

Use the worksheets at the end of this chapter to work through the following steps to creating a personal spending plan.

Step 1. Consider the basic steps to financial freedom. A well-known adage suggests that there are three things you can do with money: spend it, save it or use it to make more money. Basic financial competency involves deciding how much of your money to spend, to save and to invest so that you can be the most free with your time and generous with your resources. The following seven sequential steps provide a simple guide for moving from financial urgency and stress to financial freedom, sustainability and generosity.

1. Pay down your credit cards and other high interest debts.

2. Create an emergency fund equal to two to four months of basic living expenses.

3. Save for upcoming short-term expenses like taxes, insurance premiums, car repairs, vehicle replacement and home repairs.

4. Buy an asset, like an affordable home, to build equity and create stability.

5. Save toward longer-term financial goals like a career shift, children's education, travel or old age.

6. Invest to create a passive income stream so you are less dependent on your earnings (rental property, a business, etc.).

7. Give generously.

Step 2. Determine what financial season you are in. Recognizing which season of life you are in will help you identify appropriate financial goals. A financial decision that makes perfect sense in one season may not be wise in another. Each season of life has its own unique challenges and opportunities. Which of the following best describes the financial season you currently are in? Which describes the next season you will enter?

Discovery. You've just graduated from college, the last child has moved out, or you've recently retired from your paid work. This is a season of less responsibility and more freedom to ask questions like Who am I? What do I want be about? How do I want to spend my time? Because your financial obligations are flexible and you are less tied down, it's a season when it's safe to explore, take on new risks and discover what you want to do in a new stage of life.

Seasonal tips:

+ Invest in new experiences to gain skills and broaden your vision.

+ Minimize spending and pay down any debt you have (including student loans) so that you are free to embrace the path you discover.

+ Start saving if you anticipate that your next season of life will require increased spending or financial responsibilities (a wedding, a home, further schooling).

Preparation or transition. You are going to school, in the process of changing careers, moving from two incomes to one or starting a business. Or you are saving toward a life milestone like a wedding, home down payment, children's education, sabbatical or retirement. This is a season of preparation for what you anticipate happening next. Assuming that you are managing your resources reasonably well, your focus at this point can be on pursuing your deeper goals and values.

Seasonal tips:

+ If you share life with another person, it will be important to talk about and agree on your life vision, values and financial goals.

+ Focusing on deeper values and life purpose goals can keep you motivated and disciplined to work and save.

+ Remember that changing conditions, like tuition increases, job insecurity and market fluctuations, can affect the timeline of these goals, so be realistic and open to adjustment or other solutions.

Recovery. This is a season when your finances are out of balance and you need to stabilize. Many of us will be in a season of recovery at some point in our lives. You may realize that spending more than you earn has created debt and mounting stress. Or you are recovering from a financial setback: you've recently lost your job, gotten divorced, a business failed, the value of your home or investments have plummeted or you have significant medical bills to pay. It's a season when your focus should be on recovering a sense of stability and sustainability.

Seasonal tips:

→ Use this crisis as an opportunity to reevaluate your financial patterns.

→ Consider whether there is something you can do to alleviate pressure (work more hours, sell some assets, downsize your housing).

→ Do what you can to minimize expenses, pay down debts or become more financially literate.

→ Pay attention both to your financial situation and healthy ways to deal with your loss and stress.

→ Don't beat yourself up. Just take your next healthy step.

Providing. You are responsible to provide for dependent children or other family members. It's likely that there are greater housing costs, larger grocery bills, health insurance and medical costs, clothing to purchase, or childcare and education expenses. Many people in this life stage feel stretched between work and home responsibilities. It's the season that requires the greatest financial resources and the most concentrated investment of time. Your focus is on providing for the immediate needs of a family or loved ones and preparing your kids for future independence.

Seasonal tips:

→ Providing stability and presence to your family may need to become a higher priority than exploring passions, taking risks or even volunteering. It may help to remind yourself that you are in the fullness of life and that in another season you will have more freedom and spare time.

→ When life is full, it's easy to slip into consumptive patterns as a way to cope. Living by a spending plan and having clear financial goals and priorities is especially important during this stage of life.

→ This is a time when balance between work, family and self-care can seem hard to achieve, but is worth fighting for.

Giving. You have prepared for older age, most of life's major expenses like mortgage payments and children's education are behind you, and you have reached a point where you can choose to work for joy or for pay. You may have passive income from investments or retirement accounts that are more than you need to live on. Maybe you own a home or other property and the possessions that were once useful now seem unnecessary. This is a season when you are free to give away your time, wisdom and material assets toward causes and people you care about. Your focus is on leaving a meaningful legacy.

Seasonal tips:

→ As we become more financially secure and comfortable, our tendency is to become more risk averse, even though true vitality comes from continuing to grow and change. Ask yourself, What am I willing to risk and dream at this new stage of life to continue the adventure?

→ Retirement is often seen as a time to spend on ourselves. Hopefully, you haven't put off living a full and meaningful life until now. This is an opportunity to be generous with your time and resources.

→ It might be time to start paring down your possessions so that your family doesn't have to after you are gone.

→ Think about how you would like to invest in people and causes that you care about.

Which financial season are you in? Which season have you most recently passed through? What season do you see next on the horizon?

Step 3. Align your life vision and financial goals. Now its time to connect your deeper life purpose and values with concrete financial goals. Look back at the purpose statement and one-year goals you developed in chapter one. Keeping your financial season and these goals in mind, think through specific financial goals for the next one to three years. In each of the following areas, list or mark what you think are appropriate next steps.

Spending/Giving

☐ Learn to live by a budget and utilize money management tools.

☐ Minimize and simplify monthly expenses.

☐ Curb compulsive spending.

☐ Set voluntary limits on consumption.

☐ Give away at least 10 percent of income.

☐ Implement a graduated tithe by increasing giving by 1 percent a year.

☐ Transition to ethical, slave-free and green spending practices (even when these goods are more costly).

☐ Clarify a strategy for legacy giving.

☐ Other:_____

Debt Reduction

☐ Find out the total owed to all creditors.

☐ Make a plan for paying down debts.

☐ Sell items and property that are unnecessary or extravagant, and use proceeds to pay off debts.

☐ Seek loan forgiveness, reduction or consolidation.

☐ Pay off high-interest consumer debts.

☐ Pay down school loans.

☐ Make additional payments to mortgage principal.

☐ Other:_____

Work and Earning

☐ Obtain higher paying work or work with better benefits.

☐ Move from part-time to full-time employment.

☐ Transition to a job or career that is more meaningful or more fully utilizes skills.

☐ Move from a two-income to a one-and-a-half or a one-income household.

☐ Implement a passive income stream (e.g., rental property).

☐ Develop a home-based business (child or elder care, home or car repair, vintage book sales).

☐ Other:_____

Saving

☐ Set aside $_____ for upcoming fixed expenses (insurance, taxes, car repairs, home maintenance).

☐ Set aside $_____ (2-4 months income) in an emergency fund (job loss, unexpected repairs, medical expenses).

☐ Save $_____/mo. for next vehicle purchase.

☐ Save $_____/mo. for travel.

☐ Save $_____/mo. for continuing education or children's education.

☐ Save $_____/mo. for mortgage down payment.

☐ Save $_____/mo. for _____

☐ Other:_____

Investing

☐ Contribute $_____/mo. to a retirement account.

☐ Save $_____/mo. toward the purchase of a rental property or business.

☐ Transition banking and investments to ethical and green institutions.

☐ Intentionally invest in companies that create jobs in emerging markets and support ethical and sustainable global development.

☐ Other:_____

Step 4. List all your sources of income and estimate your monthly and yearly earnings. In addition to salary and other earnings you will want to include things like mileage reimbursement, side jobs and even gifts. You want to be aware of the variety of ways that you are being provided for. If you don't include all sources of income you will have a less accurate accounting of how you are being provided for—and might be tempted to spend funds that may be needed for essential expenses.

While this won't be part of your spending plan, we believe it's helpful to note the estimated value of what might be normal out-of-pocket expenses that are provided for you through another source (e.g., you receive a scholarship or someone else pays for your cell phone or your employer provides your health insurance). It's also helpful to note any goods or services you receive at a reduced rate. These are important to value because if your situation changes, you may have to pay for these expenses out of pocket.

Step 5. List your estimated essential and flexible expenses. Think through all the categories of your normal spending, beginning with essential fixed expenses like charitable giving, taxes, housing and food, followed by discretionary expense categories like entertainment and vacation. The following are some tips on what to include in each category.

Charitable giving. We think it's a good idea to make giving the first category in your spending plan. This is a way of acknowledging that all of your financial provision ultimately comes from the Creator and that those resources have been given to you to do good and share with others.

You will want to decide what percentage of income to give away. We think 10 percent is a good baseline amount, which has a historical Judeo-Christian precedent. If that percentage currently seems like a stretch, consider implementing a graduated tithe, by starting with a certain percentage and making a commitment to increase your giving by 1 percent a year. People vary in their convictions about how or where this money should be given and whether the amount should be calculated before or after taxes. Some people give all or most of their designated percentage to a religious institution or faith community, while others distribute their giving among several organizations and causes.

In the Hebrew Scriptures, tithes (the tenth part) and voluntary offerings were used for a variety of purposes, from maintaining the temple and priesthood to providing for the poor. The Israelites were also instructed to set aside resources to celebrate three annual feasts as acts of devotion, gratitude and remembrance. One of these, Sukkot or the Festival of Tabernacles (Leviticus 23:33-43), is similar to the American Thanksgiving holiday, though far more lengthy and extravagant. In the early church money was voluntarily offered to care for the poor, to help those living under persecution and to fund traveling teachers and emissaries.

Our family divides our giving into four subcategories. We think it's important to give toward the common work of our faith community. There are also several issues of local and global need that we are passionate about, so a portion of our giving goes to those organizations and projects. We also want to celebrate life and offer hospitality to others, so a portion of our giving goes to hosting meals and feasts to share with our friends, neighbors and extended families. In addition to this giving, we also plan a certain percentage of income for gift-giving among our family and friends.

Income taxes. If you make money, you are likely required to pay taxes. Although most of us want to pay as little tax as possible and we don't always agree with how our tax money is spent, the fact is that we benefit from and participate in a governmental system that is mandated with providing roads, schools, libraries, public health and safety, and the like. When questioned about taxes, Jesus once said, "Give back to Caesar what is Caesar's and to God what is God's"

Homemade Presents
Hailey Scandrette

As a kid I always loved giving gifts. Birthdays and Christmas were times for merrily busying myself with coming up with the perfect present for a certain friend or relative. We often made our own gifts at home; an art box with specialized supplies decorated with things my friend liked, a homemade pencil case and journal cover that I embroidered puppies on for my dog-loving friend, or a batch of my uncle's favorite treats for Christmas. My mom is a fellow lover of gift-giving and always put an extraordinary amount of time and thought into helping us prepare gifts for our friends and family. We didn't always have a large budget for presents, so it made sense to put time into them instead of money. I know many of my friends worry that homemade presents aren't as nice, but I know that my friend, Vivi, still has the quilt I made her when we were twelve. And I just can't get rid of the paint-covered canvas my brother Isaiah so excitedly gave me when he was six. Homemade presents may not be as polished or perfect, but to me, they are much more valuable than any expensive present I've ever received.

(Mark 12:17). We should each pay our fair share. For budgeting purposes it is fairly easy to estimate the amount of your yearly taxes by looking at your previous year's tax bill. You will want to make sure you are taking the proper amount of exemptions so that you don't underpay or overpay. If you are self-employed, you will want to make appropriate quarterly estimated tax payments.

Food and household supplies. All food-related expenses and household supplies, like laundry soap and toilet paper, are included in this category. We also use a couple of subcategories to track and monitor our spending on luxury items like tea, coffee and wine—

where we might be tempted to overspend. We don't include restaurant meals in this category because for us dining out is either an entertainment or business expense.

Health care. Health care includes any out-of-pocket medical-related expenses like health insurance, doctor copayments, prescriptions, over-the-counter medications, vitamins and preventative care like a gym or weight-loss-club membership.

Housing and utilities. In the utilities category you want to list all expenses related to housing, including rent, mortgage, utilities, property taxes, insurance and maintenance costs.

Transportation. For transportation, list all expenses related to local transportation, including fuel, insurance, vehicle registration and repairs. Don't forget to include tolls and parking. We live in a city with very stringent, and perhaps predatory, parking regulations, so we include the cost of at least one parking ticket in our yearly spending plan.

Childcare and education. List any expenses related to childcare and education, including child support payments and adoption costs.

Debt repayment. If you have consumer debt or school loans, list those monthly payments under debt repayment.

Forecast savings. Next, you will want to list any forecasted savings goals, like vehicle replacement costs, home repairs, health insurance deductibles and emergency funds. These are not necessarily current expenses but big-ticket amounts that you are likely to need in the future related to essential spending categories. If you own a home remember to include larger long-term maintenance costs like a new roof or furnace. This doubles as a reference for designated savings. We recommend having the equivalent of two to four months income designated to this account.

Just looking at the lump sum in your savings or checking account you might think, Wow, I have money to spend on whatever I want. Designating savings is a good way to keep you motivated and disciplined to save toward forecasted expenses and longer-term financial goals. We have the total amount in this spending category automati-

Waiting Patiently, Working Hard
Hailey Scandrette

When I was five my parents started giving me an allowance of $1 per week. Unless it was a holiday or birthday our parents didn't buy us toys, so we had two options: we could spend our dollar immediately on little trinkets like bouncy balls or marbles; or we could save our money until we had enough to buy a nice toy that we wanted. I decided I wanted an American Girl doll, which at the time cost $84. I saved for a year, didn't spend any of my allowance and asked relatives for money toward my doll for my birthday. By the time I turned six I'd saved enough, and I bought myself my own "Kirsten" doll. I felt so proud. Most of my friends who had American Girl dolls had been given them by their grandparents or other relatives, but I'd managed to buy mine all by myself. I noticed that my doll was almost always better taken care of than the dolls of my friends. I realized this was because my doll was a prized possession that I'd waited patiently for and worked hard to save up the money to buy.

cally transferred from our checking to our savings account each month.

The preceding items are your basic and essential expenses—the minimum monthly amount you need to stay financially solvent. These are your highest-priority budget items. Now list your non-essential/flexible expenses. The following spending categories are for less essential and more flexible expenses. We recommend that you only fund these categories after essential spending areas have been covered by your earnings.

Clothing. We have a clothing budget for each person in our family and designate a monthly amount for each person based on anticipated need. For instance, when a child is growing rapidly we allocate more of our spending to his or her clothing.

Personal allowances. We provide a modest amount of discretionary fun money to each person in our family to spend however they choose. We think that even when income is quite low, it's a good idea to have a little bit of walking-around money.

Communication. Depending on your lifestyle, you might consider this expense an essential category. Here we include Internet access, phone services and news magazines—any expenses related to staying connected to people and information.

Travel and entertainment. We use the travel and entertainment category for things like eating at restaurants, going to movies, concerts or shows, and travel for family vacations or to see relatives. (Depending on your family, visiting relatives may or may not be the same as taking a vacation.)

Durable household goods. In the durable household goods category we include things like furniture, appliances, kitchenware, tools and home decoration. Usually we only spend money on these items with excess funds from the previous year's income.

Long-term savings. Long-term savings includes money for a home down payment, old-age funds or passive income investing.

Business expenses and reimbursements. Some people track their business-related expenses and report them as deductions on their yearly taxes. Or these expenses can be reimbursed by a company or employer. It can be tricky dealing with reimbursable work-related expenses like travel, meals and supplies. We recommend that you keep these expenses as separate as possible from your personal finances. The best arrangement, which is not always an option, is to ask your employer to provide you with a business credit card that is paid by the company. The next best option is to keep a separate credit card for reimbursable business-related expenses. You can use the monthly statements to create your expense reports. For many people the challenge with reimbursements is to turn in reports on time so that your personal funds aren't tied up with business expenses. You will also want to make sure you have an amount reserved in your checking or savings to cover these expenses so that you don't incur credit card interest charges.

Step 6. Balance your spending plan. After you've identified monthly and yearly amounts for each category, the next step is to balance your spending plan. You do this by subtracting your total expenses from the amount of your projected income. Is what you have designated to spend more or less than what you anticipate earning? If your planned spending is greater than your anticipated earning, go back through your spending plan to see if there are any categories where you can reduce or eliminate spending. Consider whether there might be creative ways to increase your earnings or decrease your expenses in certain spending categories. (For tips on maximizing your resources, see chapter six.)

Creating a spending plan provides a good opportunity to revisit and clarify your deeper purpose and life goals. Your spending plan, to a greater extent, is a manifestation of what you value and where you find satisfaction and purpose. The following are some questions you may want to consider:

+ Am I living within my means and paying down my debts?

+ Am I spending in ways that reflect contentment, generosity and an awareness of global needs?

+ Am I moving toward financial sustainability—preparing for old age or a time when I may earn less than I am right now?

+ Does my time reflect a sustainable rhythm of work, rest, service and relationships?

+ Does my present work utilize my gifts and express my passions to do good?

Step 7. Implement your spending plan. Now that you've created a balanced spending plan, the next important step is to decide how to keep on target with your plan. This is where the rubber meets the road. The more simple and clear your strategy is, the better. For each category in your spending plan you'll want to decide how those expenses will be paid, either by cash, check, debit card, credit card or automatic payment.

Automatic payments. Automatic payments are a good option for your regular expenses like housing, utilities, insurance and telephone. Most banks offer online banking services that include free automatic electronic check payments. You can even set up your credit cards on autopay to make sure that you pay them off on time every month. You still need to check to see that the amounts billed are accurate and to confirm that payments have been sent. It may take a couple of hours to set up automatic payments and electronic billing, but it's well worth the time saved writing checks every month and the cost of postage.

Checks. Some people are less comfortable with online banking and prefer to pay their bills by check. If you choose this option you'll need to develop a monthly schedule for when you will sit down to pay your bills and balance your check book.

Debit or credit cards. Debit or credit cards are a good option for flexible expenditures like fuel, car repairs and airline tickets that are in your spending plan, provided that you pay off any balances at the end of each month. But it's also easy to swipe a debit or credit card and lose track of the total amount you've spent. For this reason we suggest you use these cards only for a limited number of spending categories—especially if you have a history of overspending with credit cards. We use credit cards exclusively for car and travel expenses, major appliances and online purchases. If you have a history of overspending with credit cards you may want to use a debit card instead.

Cash. Cash is easy to spend and difficult to track. Have you ever gone to the ATM and taken out $200 and later tried to remember where you spent it all? We recommend you use an envelope cash-budgeting method and limit your cash spending to just three or four categories: food, entertainment, clothing and personal allowance. In a two-person household you'll also want to decide who carries what cash. I know that if I have cash in my wallet, it's either for entertainment or my personal allowance, and I keep these in separate compartments. Lisa keeps our food money and her personal allowance in separate compartments of her purse. We only use cash for those specific spending categories and take out the designated amounts at the beginning of each month. When the cash is gone, we know there's nothing more to spend in that category. Choosing to live by a spending plan will require you to say no to wants, delay gratification and exercise self-control over impulse purchases.

Examine the spending plan you've developed, and for each category, using the third column of the worksheet, indicate what method you plan to use to pay for each expenditure (autopay, cash, check, debit or credit card).

The second part of implementing your spending plan is to track your spending. After you've created and balanced your spending plan, we recommend that you decide on a technique for tracking your spending. To track spending you can use budgeting software or a simple spreadsheet. Set aside a time each month to enter and calculate your earning and spending. If you are using budgeting software, you may be able to download most of the information you need from your bank and credit card company. Run a report once a month or once a quarter to see if you are on track with your spending plan and to make budgeting adjustments. You will also want to organize your financial records, have a designated place where you keep your financial papers and a monthly time when you pay current bills.

EXPERIMENT: SHARE YOUR SPENDING PLAN

Sharing your spending plan with a trusted group of friends can be a powerful way to reinforce your commitment to using your time and money to pursue what matters most. For the past seven years we've shared spending plans through a yearly meeting in our neighborhood faith community. When we first began this practice, it seemed risky. Someone suggested that we share our budgets because so many of us

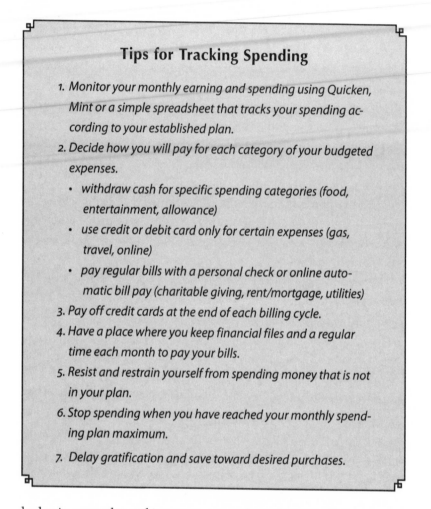

Tips for Tracking Spending

1. Monitor your monthly earning and spending using Quicken, Mint or a simple spreadsheet that tracks your spending according to your established plan.
2. Decide how you will pay for each category of your budgeted expenses.
   - withdraw cash for specific spending categories (food, entertainment, allowance)
   - use credit or debit card only for certain expenses (gas, travel, online)
   - pay regular bills with a personal check or online automatic bill pay (charitable giving, rent/mortgage, utilities)
3. Pay off credit cards at the end of each billing cycle.
4. Have a place where you keep financial files and a regular time each month to pay your bills.
5. Resist and restrain yourself from spending money that is not in your plan.
6. Stop spending when you have reached your monthly spending plan maximum.
7. Delay gratification and save toward desired purchases.

had pain, struggles and insecurity around our finances. Since we want to be a supportive and loving community to one another, it makes sense to risk sharing this part of ourselves. As you might imagine, this has been one of the most tender and intimate practices of our community, and the evening is often filled with tears and laughter.

We usually start the night by asking, What excites you or scares you about what we are about to do? For some of us it's frightening to reveal how little we make or to share about our debts or past mistakes. For others, sharing how well-off we are is intimidating, or we're afraid someone will judge our spending choices. I usually remind the group that our goal is to encourage each other to live out our deeper values through our finances and to support one another in making wise and conscious financial choices. It isn't to scrutinize each other's finances but to listen to what the Spirit is inviting each of us to do as a next step toward freedom.

We ask each person to come prepared with a spending plan similar to the worksheet at the end of this chapter. Most people come with copies of their worksheets to pass out. Others bring one copy to reference. We leave this choice up to each person, depending on how comfortable he or she is, but we encourage people to be as transparent as possible.

To give each person equal time to share, we've found it helpful to set a timer for five to seven minutes. After sharing some basic information about earning and spending, we ask each person to respond to the following questions:

→ As you created your spending plan, what stood out to you? Where did you feel the most challenged or encouraged?

→ Did this process bring up any questions you are still trying to answer?

→ What are your financial goals for this year?

→ Which of your financial goals will require the most intentional effort or discipline? Where do you recognize a particular opportunity to trust God?

After the timer rings, people are free to ask clarifying questions or to offer quick advice and encouragements. It's not uncommon for someone to say, "I have a lot of experience dealing with that issue, I'd be happy to meet with you to talk more about it later." Before moving on to the next person we ask, "What can we as a community do to help you achieve your financial goals?" and "How can we pray for you right now?"

Some people approach this practice with a lot of trepidation, but afterward most people are pleasantly surprised by how comfortable and supported they felt. Through our sharing we discover specific ways to support one another. We might find out that someone in our group needs work, is taking courageous steps to pay off debts or isn't making it financially and needs help with diapers, housing or groceries. As we've shared spending plans over the years, it's become clear that evaluating finances by the numbers is difficult because no one's situation is the same. In fact, two people can make the same amount of money and be in wildly different places financially. Or a higher-income person with fewer assets and a larger tax burden or student loans may be less free than someone with a much lower income who owns property or has lower monthly fixed expenses. Each of us is simply invited to ask, What's my next step toward becoming more free to spend my time and money on what matters most?

A spending plan doesn't put limits on your life; it's a tool to help you consciously choose what matters most to you.

> *What excites or frightens you about the possibility of sharing your spending plan with a friend or group of friends?*

TASK: FINANCIAL PLANNING WORKSHEET

The following is a worksheet form for the financial planning steps explored in this chapter. By completing this worksheet you will have a comprehensive financial plan from which to pursue your deeper values and goals in a tangible way.

Circle the current step you are on in your journey toward financial freedom.

1. Pay down credit cards and other high interest debts.

2. Create an emergency fund equal to 2-4 months of basic living expenses.

3. Save ahead for upcoming short-term expenses (taxes, insurance premiums, car repairs, vehicle replacement, home repairs, etc.).

4. Buy an asset, like a home you can afford, to build equity and create stability.

5. Save toward longer-term financial goals like a career shift, children's education, travel or old age.

6. Invest to create passive income so you are less dependent on earning an income (rental property, a business, etc.).

7. Give generously.

FINANCIAL SEASONS

Which financial season are you in?

discovery

recovery

preparation or transition

providing

giving

Which season have you most recently passed through?

discovery

recovery

preparation or transition

providing

giving

What season do you see next on the horizon?

discovery

recovery

preparation or transition

providing

giving

What are your short-term (1-3 years) goals in the following areas of personal finance? Refer back to your responses to the step 3 exercise in this chapter and select a goal in each area.

Spending/Giving

_____

_____

Debt Reduction

_____

_____

Work and Earning

_____

_____

Saving

_____

_____

Investing

_____

_____

Spending Plan

First, list your individual financial assets (or your household assets if you are part of a family).

Checking account(s) $_____

Savings account(s) $_____

Retirement account(s) $_____

Stock and investment account(s) $_____

Value of stock options $_____

Property equity $_____

Value of vehicles $_____

Other assets $_____

Total assets $_____

Now estimate the value of what might be normal out-of-pocket expenses that (1) are provided for you through another source, or (2) that you receive at a reduced rate. The goal here is to recognize the value of indirect financial provisions to help you anticipate how new choices or circumstances would impact your spending plan.

	Monthly	Yearly
Medical benefits		
Dental benefits		
Value of employer-paid air miles		
Housing/phone/utility assistance		
Free or reduced housing		
Food stamps/free groceries		
Free access to a vacation home		
Grants and scholarships		
Free or reduced childcare		
Free or reduced counseling		
Other		
Other		
Other		
Total		

List the current streams of your individual or household income.

	Monthly	Yearly
Salary/hourly wages		
Self-employment business income		
Bank interest		
Disability, aid and retirement		
Gifts/trust fund income		
Business travel mileage reimbursement		
Investment dividends		
Employer 401(k) contributions		
Stock options		
Stock purchase plan		
Other		
Total		

SPENDING

Fill in all categories of spending that relate to your current life situation.

	Monthly	Yearly	Payment Method
Charitable Giving			
Faith community			
Global development			
Support of causes and organizations			
Hospitality			
Gifts			
Spontaneous acts of kindness			
Other _____			
Total			

	Monthly	Yearly	Payment Method

Income Tax

Federal income taxes

FICA or self-employment tax

State and local taxes

Total

Food and Household Supplies

Groceries

Household supplies

Luxury goods (coffee/tea/alcohol)

Other _____

Total

Health Care

Health insurance

Doctor/dental copayments

Medications

Preventative care

Total

Housing and Utilities

Rent/mortgage

Utilities

Gas

Electric

Water

Garbage

Property/renter's insurance

Property tax

Home maintenance/repair or HOA

Home furnishings and

improvements

Total

	Monthly	Yearly	Payment Method
Transportation			
Public transportation			
Car/bicycle maintenance & repairs			
Fuel			
Vehicle loan repayment			
Auto insurance			
Vehicle registration			
Parking, tickets, tolls and citations			
Total			
Childcare and education			
Life insurance			
Disability insurance			
Debt Repayments			
Addition to vehicle loan			
Consumer debt			
Student loans			
Private loans			
Business debt			
Addition to mortgage principal			
Total			
Forecasted Expense Savings			
Emergency cash reserve			
Vehicle replacement			
Home maintenance			
Health insurance deductible			
Total			

	Monthly	Yearly	Payment Method

Long-Term Savings and Investments

	Monthly	Yearly	Payment Method
Home down payment	_____	_____	_____
Education fund	_____	_____	_____
Passive income investment	_____	_____	_____
Old age/retirement	_____	_____	_____
Other _____	_____	_____	_____
Other _____	_____	_____	_____
Total	_____	_____	_____

Communication

	Monthly	Yearly	Payment Method
Phone(s)	_____	_____	_____
Internet Service	_____	_____	_____
Cable TV/media services	_____	_____	_____
Newspaper and magazines	_____	_____	_____
Total	_____	_____	_____

Clothing Allowance (for each person in your household)

	Monthly	Yearly	Payment Method
_____	_____	_____	_____
_____	_____	_____	_____
_____	_____	_____	_____
_____	_____	_____	_____
Total	_____	_____	_____

Personal Allowance (for each person in your household)

	Monthly	Yearly	Payment Method
_____	_____	_____	_____
_____	_____	_____	_____
_____	_____	_____	_____
_____	_____	_____	_____
Total	_____	_____	_____

	Monthly	Yearly	Payment Method
Travel and Entertainment			
Vacation/travel			
Entertainment and dining out	___	___	___
Other _____	___	___	___
Total	___	___	___
Durable Household Goods			
_____	___	___	___
_____	___	___	___
_____	___	___	___
Total	___	___	___
Total Expenses	___	___	___
Business-Related Expenses			
Business travel	___	___	___
Business entertainment	___	___	___
Business supplies & clothing	___	___	___
Other _____	___	___	___
Total	___	___	___

BALANCE YOUR SPENDING PLAN

	Monthly	Yearly
Projected income	___	___
Budgeted expenses	___	___
Difference	___	___

6

Maximize Your Resources

*To everyone who has, more will be given, but as for the one who
has nothing, even what they have will be taken away.*

LUKE 19:26

For most of us, pursuing our dreams, living within our means and
following a spending plan that reflects long-term sustainability will
require frugality, minimizing waste and maximizing resources. At the
heart of frugality is a spiritual principle, "Whoever can be trusted
with very little can also be trusted with much" (Luke 16:10). Jesus
said that learning to manage our money and material possessions well
prepares us to handle the "true riches" of living in the present reality
of God's kingdom. "If you have not been trustworthy in handling
worldly wealth, who will trust you with true riches?" (Luke 16:11).

Practicing frugality can help you stay within your spending plan
and give you more resources to be generous with. And the practice of
frugality can help you become less wasteful, reducing your global
footprint and consumption of natural resources to pioneer a more

sustainable lifestyle for future generations. What's good for the soul is good for the pocketbook and also the planet. In this chapter we'll explore skills for maximizing and economizing your resources that can help you be more free to spend your time and money on what matters most.

THINK CREATIVELY

Practicing frugality involves learning to think creatively and resourcefully. Necessity, as they say, is the mother of invention. With a bit of ingenuity many of life's necessities can be provided more cheaply, and it can be fun to search for alternatives to the conventional ways that goods and services are purchased. It can help to have some questions in mind to expand your imagination:

→ Is this the only way?

→ Is there a cheaper way?

→ Do I have other choices?

→ How would my great-grandmother have done this?

A few years ago our kitchen was in need of renovation. When we bought the house, the kitchen needed an upgrade, but it wasn't the top priority in our spending plan and we weren't willing to go into debt to get the job done. We knew that it was finally time to remodel our kitchen when one of the cupboards fell off the wall. It would have cost $25,000 or more to hire a contractor, so we decided to do it ourselves. Even to do it ourselves we estimated needing to spend $15,000 in materials, but we only had $5,000 saved toward the renovation. So we explored creative alternatives. On Craigslist I (Mark) found a couple who wanted to completely gut and remodel the kitchen in the five-year-old house they just bought. They were willing to sell us the cabinets, stove, oven, microwave and dishwasher for $1,200. We also found a slightly used energy-efficient refrigerator for $300, which I was able to pick up at the same time with the rental truck. Our boys helped me tear out the old kitchen, and with the help of my dad and a few friends I installed the cabinets, plumbing and countertops and retiled the floor. Lisa tiled the backsplash and together as a family we repainted the ceiling and walls. We hired an electrician to do the work we weren't qualified to do ourselves and spent a total of $4,000. This took some weekends, a week of vacation time and some patience to live in a construction zone for several months. And we made a few compromises on materials, like installing Formica rather than stone countertops. But some creativity and elbow grease allowed us to get the new kitchen we needed without going into debt while reusing materials wherever possible.

For starters, economizing might mean questioning your normal spending patterns.

→ Do I really need this latte? Could I learn to make this at home, or would I be just as happy with a regular cup of coffee?

→ I spend hundreds of dollars every two months on a haircut, dye and styling. Maybe it's time for a more natural look.

→ By the time we've ordered a salad, an appetizer, drinks and entrees for the two of us, we've spent $75-100, not including tip. We've got to find a cheaper way to enjoy ourselves at a restaurant.

Here's a situation to which a little creativity could be applied. Occasionally we are invited to spend time with a group of people who decide to go out to dinner. So, ten or fifteen of us will wait forty-five minutes to an hour to be seated in a noisy restaurant. Everyone is jammed together at long tables that limit conversation, and we're all distracted by trying to get our orders in. For some the restaurant may be too expensive, but they come along and spend money they don't have because they want to be included. In our experience we have had a better time when we go to someone's home or apartment for food and drinks. When someone is willing to host and offer hospitality, fifteen people can easily feast to their hearts' content for about the same amount as four restaurant meals. It just takes some foresight and creativity.

A CLOSER LOOK AT LARGER EXPENSES

For most people the largest yearly expenses are housing, utilities, Social Security, food, transportation, health care, education and debt maintenance. Let's look more closely at these spending categories to see what steps might be taken to minimize these expenses.

Housing. Most of us spend an average of one-third of our income on housing, making it our single largest expense. In some housing markets it is actually closer to 50 percent. If you are in a position to do so, often it can be cheaper to buy than to rent a home, though buying a home requires a down payment, a longer-term commitment and ongoing maintenance costs. You might choose to reduce your housing expenses by relocating to a smaller or more affordable home or apartment. If that's not feasible, you could also look for an opportunity to share housing with others or rent out part of your home to a friend. We know of families who have chosen to live with parents or their adult children and grandchildren. This is a typical economizing strategy for immigrant families. It might make a valid option for more of us as housing prices continue to rise.

There are some expenses in our society that are difficult to afford without borrowing—including buying a home. We recommend that you shop for a home that you can realistically afford on one income, even if your monthly income dropped significantly. Many people borrow money for a home assuming that in the future their income will go up or the value of the home will increase. But the recent real estate crash proved, with many mortgages going "upside down," that we can't reliably predict what the value of that home will be in the future. You can also minimize your risk by buying a property that includes an additional rental unit, using the rental income to make the mortgage payment or pay down the loan more quickly. When you do take out a home mortgage, it's preferable to put at least 20 percent down to avoid private mortgage insurance, which, depending on your loan amount, can add up to hundreds of dollars a month and thousands of dollars a year in additional costs.

Some questions to keep in mind when you are shopping for a home:

→ Is the amount I am financing low enough that I will still be able to make the payment even if I experience a drop in income?

→ Is the house in a location where I am likely to be able to sell it quickly if I decide to move?

→ If I need to move away or have a loss of income, could the house be rented out at an amount that would cover the mortgage, taxes and maintenance?

Social security. Most US workers pay 7.65 percent of their income into the Federal Insurance Contributions Act (or FICA) toward old-age pension and medical care (up to a certain income level). Your employer pays a matching 7.65 percent. If you are self-employed, you pay 15.3 percent of self-employment earnings through quarterly estimated payments. There isn't much you can do to reduce this expenditure, except to make sure that you are not overpaying. If you are claiming the proper number of deductions, you shouldn't get a refund or have to make additional payments when you file your yearly tax return.

Food. On average, Americans spend less on food than most developed countries (9-12 percent of income). American food costs are artificially low because of farm subsidies for commodities like corn.[1] Dining out accounts for almost 40 percent of the money spent on food. When Lisa and I were first married we spent just $90 a month on food. Even in 1991 that was not a lot of money to feed two people and multiple weekly dinner guests for an entire month. Today we spend half of what our local food bank suggests is the minimum amount needed to feed a family our size. How do we do it? We buy what's in season, in quantity and prepare our meals at home using whole foods and fresh ingredients. It is almost always more economical to prepare food yourself than to buy processed food or eat at

---

[1]Mark Sisson, "What Is the Cost of Eating Healthy Foods?" *Mark's Daily Apple (blog),* March 9, 2012, www.marksdailyapple.com/what-is-the-cost-of-eating-healthy-foods/#axzz25LtW08q0.

a restaurant, and it's often a healthier and more earth-friendly option. With a knowledge of basic cooking techniques and a few good kitchen tools, it can be quicker, tastier and more satisfying to cook at home than to eat out. You can also conserve time and work by preparing multiple meals at the same time, putting one meal in the freezer or in the refrigerator to reheat for lunches.

Simple Ways to Reduce Food Costs

1. Cook most of your meals at home using fresh ingredients.
2. Primarily buy whole foods (dairy, proteins, fruits, vegetables and grains).
3. Avoid buying processed and prepared foods that are more expensive, unhealthy or calorie intensive.
4. Buy staple food items at your local farmer's market or grocery store when they are in season or on sale.
5. Buy foods in quantity. Food is often cheaper when bought in bulk. But be careful not to buy more than you need or let it go to waste.
6. Adopt a less meat-dependent diet by learning to prepare tasty plant protein meals at least some of the time.
7. Cook in quantity. You can save money and time by preparing larger amounts of food for multiple meals.
8. Pack a lunch for work using leftovers and staples from your refrigerator and cupboards.
9. Make more expensive food items an occasional luxury rather than normal staples of your diet (e.g., artisan cheeses, prepared snacks, etc.).
10. For many of us it would be cheaper and healthier if we simply chose to eat less.

Utilities. You can conserve spending and reduce waste by paying attention to your heating, cooling, water and electrical usage. Utility costs can fluctuate significantly depending on your household usage patterns. The following are some earth-friendly ways to reduce utility costs.

+ Invest in energy efficient appliances and light bulbs.
+ Take shorter and less frequent showers.
+ Don't leave water running while you wash dishes or brush your teeth.
+ Use heating and air conditioning less frequently or at more moderate settings.
+ Air dry clothes.
+ Turn off lights and unplug appliances when not in use.

Transportation. Traveling the open road is often seen as a birthright in the American imagination, but it is a privilege that comes at great cost, reinforcing our dependence on depleting fossil fuels and foreign oil. Here are a few ideas on reducing your transportation costs.

+ Adopt a more local lifestyle by staying in your neighborhood and buying locally if possible.
+ Reduce miles driven by carpooling and consolidating errands.
+ Share a car and vehicle expenses with a friend, or if you live in a larger city, join a city car share program.
+ Use public transportation.
+ Walk or bicycle to places that are within walking or biking distance.
+ If possible schedule meetings or find work that is a shorter distance from home.

Health care. For many people rising health insurance premiums and treatment costs are a great concern. Conventional wisdom suggests that the best way to reduce health care costs is through preventative care—by adopting a healthy and active lifestyle. In addition to this, the following are a few other recommendations.

→ See if you are getting the best deal you can on health insurance. If you are reasonably healthy, it may be better to buy insurance with a higher deductible and lower yearly premiums. You can put the money you save aside to pay your deductible if you become ill.

→ Get a yearly physical to detect health concerns early.

→ Question whether expensive additional tests are necessary.

→ Seek alternative treatment options when appropriate. We have several friends without dental insurance who have gone to Mexico for major dental work because it is a third of the cost for the equivalent domestic treatment.

→ In the United States a disproportionate amount of medical costs are for the last year or the last days of life. Invasive efforts to prolong the life of the aged are perhaps misplaced, contributing to rising health care costs. We may need to become more thoughtful about our personal end-of-life treatment choices.

Education. A lot has changed since most parents went to college, making decisions about paying for higher education of greater consequence. Over the past thirty years the cost of higher education in the United States has increased at four times the rate of inflation.[2] The current average cost for a four-year in-state bachelor's degree, including room and board, is $71,440. The average cost of a private college or university degree is $158,072.[3] While those with bachelor's degrees can expect to earn significantly more in their lifetime than

[2]Michelle Jamrisko and Ilan Kolet, "Cost of College Degree in U.S. Soars 12 Fold: Chart of the Day," *Bloomberg.com,* August15, 2012, www.bloomberg.com/news/2012-08-15/cost-of -college-degree-in-u-s-soars-12-fold-chart-of-the-day.html.
[3]"Published Tuition and Fee and Room and Board Charges, 2012-13," College Board Advocacy and Policy Center, accessed December 10, 2012, http://trends.collegeboard.org /college-pricing/figures-tables/published-prices-national#Published Tuition and Fee and Room and Board Charges, 2012-13.

those without, those advantages are offset by the increasing costs of higher education. In 2011 two-thirds of college seniors who graduated had student loans with the average student owing $26,600.[4] Parents and students have to be creative, shrewd and resourceful to minimize the expenses of college.

Amanda, the daughter of parents who immigrated to the United States shortly before she was born, told me that she hopes to be the first person in her family to graduate from college. Her dream is to be a medical missionary or aid worker in refugee camps. Both of her parents work service-level jobs and are not able to contribute to her college expenses. Through the encouragement of her youth pastor, Amanda has applied to a four-year private Christian university in Southern California. She believes that the training she can receive at this school, which costs $41,000 a year, is what she needs to pursue the life she's called to. Even after scholarships and financial aid Amanda will need to borrow $25,000 a year in federal loans and will be $100,000 in debt by the time she graduates. She also hopes to meet "a quality guy" at the school who shares her concerns about global poverty and will support her to be a full-time mom when they have kids someday. If the young man she hopes to marry has also taken out similar loan amounts, they will graduate and begin their life together $200,000 in debt—the equivalent of a thirty-year mortgage in many parts of the country. Amanda will have to be incredibly focused and disciplined to pay off her school loans if she is going to continue to pursue her dreams.

When I suggested that Amanda consider attending a two-year community college first, or go to a more affordable public university, she quickly dismissed these options. "I visited the campus and really liked it. They have a good nursing program. I prayed about it and just believe God wants me to go there." When asked, Amanda told me she has no experience in a medical setting and has never visited the Two-

---

[4]"Average Student Debt Climbs to $26,600 for Class of 2011," Institute for College Access and Success, accessed December 10, 2012, www.ticas.org/pub_view.php?idx=865.

Thirds World. Eighteen-year-old Amanda is about to borrow $100,000 based on a vague notion of her interests and calling—a very expensive hunch that will shape the direction of her life and possibly limit her freedom to do what she feels passionate about.

Amanda's decision-making process is not uncommon and could apply equally to someone pursuing a degree in engineering, education or the arts. Here are a few things Amanda and her parents, or someone in a similar situation, might consider before making this important decision:

1. Before Amanda decides to study nursing, it would be helpful for her to get some experience volunteering in a hospital or clinic so she can discern whether she enjoys that profession. Late adolescence can be an important time to learn through real-world experiences of work and service.

2. Before committing to a school Amanda and her parents could research scholarships and financial aid, calculate the cost and decide what they can afford. Unless Amanda receives adequate scholarships or aid, it might be wise to consider choosing an in-state public university. If that school is within commuting distance, she can even live at home, eliminating the costs of room and board.

3. If Amanda lives at home, works a part-time job and spends carefully, it's possible that she could complete her degree debt free or with minimal loans that wouldn't significantly limit her choices in the future. Even if parents are able to pay for their child's education, having their student pay a portion of the cost can foster a sense of responsibility and ownership.

Debt-maintenance. Debt-maintenance is one area for economizing that is often overlooked. One of the most critical financial decisions a person can make is the choice of whether to take on debt. Predatory credit card companies, university admissions offices and even parents often encourage taking on debt as a way to pay for larger expenses or to build a healthy credit score. Unfortunately this often occurs before a person has the skills or understanding to fully appreciate the ramifications of these decisions.

Debt is so ingrained in our culture that it's hard for many of us to imagine not taking on debt to buy a car, pay for unanticipated expenses or obtain the possessions and experiences that are associated with the good life. Looking around, it might be easy to conclude that most people are more well-off than you—driving fancier cars, owning dream homes, and enjoying meals, clothes and vacations. These signs of prosperity and luxury can be deceptive and are often financed by borrowing.

I recently attended a party at a friend's hillside home, where I was tempted to be envious of the cars in the driveway, beautiful modern architecture, nice landscaping and the fine wine and food served. Earlier my friend had told me he was thinking of selling his business to live a quieter life in the country as a gentleman farmer. At the party when I asked him about his emerging dream, he shrugged despondently, "I don't think it will ever happen." When I asked why he told me, "The company hasn't done well for several years, so we refinanced our home to cover expenses. At this point, we owe far more than the house and the company are worth. I'll be dead before I ever pay off these debts."

Because we live in society where credit is readily accessible, it's easy for us to see debt as the solution to our immediate problems, needs and wants, compounding our struggles with contentment. When we borrow for things we can't afford, we leverage our future. Debt isn't always avoidable or necessarily unwise, but it can be a consequence of a lack of contentment or creativity. As you learn to live from a sense of abundance, being grateful, trusting and content with what you already have, you will be less likely to make impatient choices that put you in debt.

Sometimes we get into debt because of a legitimate crisis or urgent need, like a plane ticket to a funeral or bus ticket for a relative getting out of drug treatment. Sometimes we end up with debt because we felt vulnerable and didn't think there were any other options. "The doctor prescribed all of these tests and at the time we thought the

condition was serious, but now we have $100,000 in medical bills."
Sometimes we get into debt because we long for comfort. "When I
broke up with my boyfriend seven years ago, I felt lonely and de-
pressed, so I booked a tropical vacation I couldn't afford and am still
paying for it." Or we get tired of the slow computer, the rusty old car
or our outdated clothes, and think we deserve more.

"The borrower is servant to the lender" (Proverbs 22:7) is a well-
known ancient adage that speaks to the reality that when you owe
someone, to a certain degree, that person owns you. Until you pay the
person back, the freedom you have to make certain choices is limited.
Our friend Justine felt called to pursue a career in pastoral ministry,
and being a single parent with a child, she decided to take out a loan
for $150,000 to finance three years of graduate school and living ex-
penses. When she considered how long it would take her to pay back
this amount, especially on a minister's salary, she hesitated. But then
she reasoned that if she was called to this work, somehow it would all
work out. In seminary the fresh and creative approaches to ministry
and church that she learned about excited and inspired her—though
rarely do those approaches provide a large or steady paycheck. Now,
with some remorse, she feels stuck doing work she doesn't enjoy, but
she does it because it offers the better salary and benefits she needs to
pay off her loans. "I'll be fifty before I'm free to do what originally
inspired me," Justine said. "Looking back, I now see how naive I was
when I signed all those papers." Her story is all too common.

Many of us stay in soul-sucking jobs or unhealthy situations because the prospective loss of income would create a very real financial crisis. So rather than making choices from an elevated sense
of vision and purpose, we end up choosing based on urgent financial
needs or long-term financial obligations. As you take steps to minimize debt, you will be more free to act on new opportunities. There
is something peaceful and liberating about knowing that you could
change jobs, relocate to a new city or take time off to do something
restful or creative.

CALCULATING THE TRUE COST OF BORROWING

A simple definition of debt: "borrowing an amount of money to purchase something now that you promise to pay back to the lender over time, usually with interest." We pay for the privilege of using someone else's money. Depending on the terms and interest rate, the cost of borrowing can be significant. With most conventional thirty-year home mortgages a person will pay as much in interest as the original purchase price. If you finance the purchase of a $250,000 home, the actual cost will be closer to $500,000 if the loan is paid over thirty years. Current interest rates on federally financed school loans are similar. Interest rates on most credit cards are much higher (16-19% annually), with additional penalties for late and missed payments. The average American has $7,150 in consumer (credit card) debt.[5] If you pay only the minimum monthly statement on that amount at the current average interest rate of 16.89 percent it would take thirty-five years to pay off, and you would spend $15,351 in interest. As one friend put it, "Those weekly pizzas I put on my credit card ten years ago in college have become very, very expensive."

These figures assume that you are paying your monthly minimums. But if for some reason you are late or miss a payment, most loans companies will charge late fees and penalties that can triple or quadruple the amount that you owe. Read the fine print on your loan or credit card paperwork. We have a friend who took out a loan for one semester of graduate school. After the semester she decided this wasn't the right career path for her and quit. Over the next few years she was underemployed and neglected her loan payments. She now owes $40,000 in principal, interest and penalties on a $15,000 low-interest school loan. That was an expensive way to figure out what she didn't want to do with her life. Recently married, she would like to start a family and buy a home, but with her and her partner's com-

---

[5]"American Household Credit Card Debt Statistics Through 2012," NerdWallet.com, accessed December 4, 2012, www.nerdwallet.com/blog/credit-card-data/average-credit-card-debt-household/.

bined debts and credit history, they can't qualify for a loan even though they now make a good income.

Is All Debt Bad?

It's a good idea to stay out of debt and plan ahead for larger expenses. But what about buying a home, starting a business or paying for higher education? When you start a business or pay for education, you are investing in the means to create income. Borrowing money to buy a home is considered a safe debt because the asset (the home) is what guarantees the loan. If you can't make your payments, you could give the property back to the bank and the loan contract would be fulfilled—(though you might lose your down payment or equity). When you borrow money to pay for a vacation there is no asset, which makes it a poor financial choice. Taking out a loan for a vehicle is similar since it usually loses its value dramatically as soon as you drive it off the lot.

TAKING STEPS TO MINIMIZE DEBT

It's hard to even talk about the issue of debt without arousing a sense of pride or shame. Those of us who are debt free can sometimes be self-righteous and preachy. Those of us who have debts can feel defensive or defeated. We think the most helpful way to look at this is to consider whether carrying debt is hindering your freedom to live out your deeper purpose—or if the level of debt you have puts you at unnecessary risk in the event of an unforeseen life change. Here are a few recommendations for minimizing debt.

1. This may seem obvious, but, whenever possible, avoid debt in the first place. If you don't have debt, work to keep it that way. If you do have debt, work to avoid acquiring more.

2. If you have adequate income right now, it's good to pay down your debt as quickly as possible, beginning with the loan with the highest interest rate. We know many people who through discipline and intentionality have been able to pay off significant debt in a matter of months or years. Chad and Kendra were almost $150,000 in debt from their undergraduate and graduate degrees. In order to keep their options for the future open, they decided to aggressively pay down their loans. By minimizing their spending, maximizing their earnings and setting clear goals they were able to pay off their loans, becoming debt free in just over two years. By making an additional monthly payment toward the principal and thus paying off your loans early, you can save a significant amount. By paying an additional $250 to principal each month, a $150,000 thirty-year home mortgage can be paid off in eighteen years at a savings of $75,550.70.

3. If you don't have adequate income to pay down your debts, explore creative solutions. One option is to sell items or property to pay off your loans. Donovan couldn't afford to keep making payments on his four-wheel-drive truck. He decided to sell the truck to pay off the loan and take public transportation until he had saved enough to pay cash for another vehicle. Another option is to negotiate with your creditors. In most cases it would be better for a lender to get back part of their money than no money at all. In a famous parable from the Gospels, the hero of the story is a shrewd manager who negotiates a lower repayment amount for borrowers (Luke 16:1-8). Credit card and utility companies can be unscrupulous with their charges, adding fees and penalties and occasionally services that were not requested. Quite often on delinquent loans the lender has already received payments equal to the original loan amount plus

interest and the lender is charging additional fees and interest to the borrower simply because they can. It may work to get on the phone and kindly request that additional charges be removed or to ask if they will accept a lower amount paid in full to settle the account.

4. You might consider asking a friend or family member to help you pay off your high interest debts either through a gift or a private loan. In some cases we've encouraged people to ask their parents or other relatives to help pay off their debts if the parents advised or pressured their child into taking on a loan or in cases of abuse, when the actions of a family member precipitated the need for medical or psychological care.

5. Obviously a gift or low-interest loan from a family member has its advantages and drawbacks. We know of situations where gifts and loans within families (or among friends) have been beautiful expressions of interdependence. Yet a loan or gift rarely comes without some strings attached. The family member may want to see evidence that you are fully committed to avoiding unnecessary debt in the future. And not paying back the loan could potentially shift the dynamics of the relationship. Perhaps we would be more careful, conscientious and responsible about our choices if we could only borrow money from people we have relationships with rather than from large and impersonal financial institutions.

6. Filing for bankruptcy protection can sometimes be the only viable option. Bankruptcy laws are written as a concession to protect borrowers from creditors when, due to extreme hardship, they have no foreseeable means of paying down their debt. In most cases a certain amount of the debt still has to be paid.

STRATEGIES FOR MAXIMIZING YOUR RESOURCES

The following are strategies you might consider using to live more resourcefully.

Choose smaller. A smaller economy car costs less to buy and repair, is cheaper to drive and better for the environment than a larger one. A two-bedroom home or apartment is cheaper than a three-bedroom home—unless, of course, you are sharing it with someone else and splitting the costs. When we were in Europe recently we discovered that a small American style cup of coffee is equal to three portions served in Norway. In a culture where more is often thought of as better, it's easy to feel pressure to go bigger and spend more. An easy way to economize is to resist the urge to supersize (unless, of course, you are sharing).

Make or do it yourself. If you have the time and the curiosity to learn, there are many ways to economize on services you might normally pay for. You could learn to cut hair, bake your own bread or roast your own coffee. You might enjoy learning to make your own soap or grow your own vegetables.

Fix or repair it. We can extend the life of many of our possessions by learning to fix or repair them. Tired of calling an appliance repair person and spending hundreds of dollars every time someone left a few pennies or a screw in the laundry, Lisa learned how to fix our washing machine herself. She is especially proud that she learned how to repair our refrigerator, using the diagnostic repair manual online, inexpensive replacement parts and a few hours of her time. Of course you have to decide what repairs you are willing to learn to do yourself and if, in the long run, it would be better to hire an expert for some jobs. We've found that to be true, for instance, with most car repairs.

Plan ahead. Sometimes urgency is costly. It starts to snow and you suddenly need a winter jacket. You get to the office and realize you haven't had breakfast. With many things, like purchasing airline tickets, planning ahead can save a lot of money.

Wait to buy and buy on sale. It also helps if you are willing to wait to buy until you find an item you need on sale or at your target price. Sometimes by waiting you also find that you don't actually need or want the item.

Buy used. You can save a lot and prolong the lifespan of a manufactured item if you are willing to buy used clothing, furniture and other household items. Over the past fifteen years we've been able to buy most of our clothes, except for socks and underwear, at thrift stores and resale shops.

Trade, borrow and share. Life is cheaper when we learn to depend on one another. Tools can be shared among neighbors. Clothes can be swapped. Many of our friends even share automobiles. When we travel we usually stay with friends. Likewise, we have guests at our house thirty or forty nights a year.

Enjoy what's free. We've learned to enjoy the opportunities that are available in our neighborhood and city—like picnics in the park, free concerts and other cultural opportunities. In most cities museums have a monthly free day.

Scavenge and reuse. Our affluent society wastes much edible food and casts off useful items. Many of us think of ourselves as above using what someone else has discarded. But if we are going to live more sustainably, we may need to begin to see castoffs and trash as more valuable commodities. Grocery stores and bakeries often throw out day-old bread that can be used and shared. In many cities people put food, clothes and household items they no longer want or need out on the street for others to pick up.

In Hebrew tradition it was common practice to leave the edges of fields unharvested for immigrants, travelers and the poor to glean from (Leviticus 19:9). We wonder if dumpster diving is the contemporary equivalent to the gleanings of the ancient poor. Perhaps you've thought those things should be left for the truly poor. In a society as wealthy and wasteful as ours, there is more thrown out than even the poor can possibly use. Personally we find a significant amount of our clothes laying on the street and regularly find discarded day-old bread in front of our neighborhood bakeries. We take what we need and share the bounty with friends and neighbors.

> *Which would be harder for you, to leave gleanings or to take gleanings?*
>
> *What thoughts or feelings come up for you as you entertain the invitation to dumpster dive?*

Negotiate on price. We weren't happy with the amount we were spending each month for Internet access. A friend suggested that I call the service provider and kindly ask them to lower our monthly rate to the currently advertised "sale" price. When I called, I was surprised how willing they were to honor my request, no questions asked, which saved us $200 over six months. We have friends who have even used this strategy to lower their monthly rent. It's often advantageous to a landlord to keep good tenants rather than search for new ones. You might also consider checking to see if you are getting the best rate on your health, home and car insurance. Make sure you aren't overinsured and do the calculations to see if it would be more economical in the long run to pay a higher deductible and lower monthly premiums.

Buy quality. It's often better to do your research and spend the extra money on items of quality that will last longer and hold their value. On occasion we've had to learn this the hard way. Once we got a great deal on a minivan that was just a few years old. That particular model had a bad maintenance track record, but we couldn't resist the deal. Over the year that we owned the minivan, we spent $8,000 in repairs before discovering that the transmission also needed to be replaced at a cost of $3,000. Our "great deal" cost as much as we would have spent on a brand-new vehicle—which we bought the next year; it has run for seven years now without a breakdown or repair.

Beware of the dark side. Frugality can have a dark side. There's a difference between being resourceful and being cheap. The quest for the best deal can be just as enticing, greedy, consumptive and materialistic as an addiction to frivolous spending. Frugality can be expensive if, for instance, you spend four hours trying to save ten dollars on a purchase. The goal of frugality is to minimize the amount of money and time spent on less important matters so you are more free to be generous. We know that frugality has gone too far when it interferes with our relationships or when being shrewd becomes an excuse to judge others and their choices.

Spend where it counts. If you are frugal in most areas, you may be able to afford to spend more on what gives you considerable pleasure. Maybe you like to travel or enjoy going to concerts. Is it the meal or dessert that you most enjoy? When it comes to entertainment, think about what is special to you and economize on things that don't bring you as much satisfaction. Some people love to see a new film in the theater on opening day, while others of us are content to watch it on DVD six months later. We don't go out to eat often, but about once a year on our anniversary or at Christmas we'll go to an award-winning restaurant, usually for lunch, to celebrate. Know what you like and spend where it counts.

We've been groomed to think that it's no longer possible to cover basic expenses or raise a family without two incomes or a significant amount of debt. But much of this is based on our assumptions about what are necessities and what constitutes a good life. If the good life means a large home, new cars, private schools and expensive hobbies and recreation, then, yes, two incomes or significant debts are necessary. But if the good life is simple enjoyments, purposeful work and meaningful relationships, then these are realistic and achievable for almost anyone who seeks to eliminate waste and maximize their resources so they are free to spend their time and money on what matters most.

TASK: ECONOMIZING
List one economizing step you would like to take in each of these larger ticket spending categories.

1. Housing: _____

2. Utilities: _____

3. Social security: _____

4. Food: _____

5. Transportation: _____

6. Health care: _____

7. Education: _____

8. Debt maintenance: _____

TASK: MAKE A PLAN FOR REDUCING AND ELIMINATING DEBT

List and calculate your current debts.

Consumer debt (credit cards)

_____ Principal: ____ Monthly payment ____ Rate: ____ Term: ____

_____ Principal: ____ Monthly payment ____ Rate: ____ Term: ____

_____ Principal: ____ Monthly payment ____ Rate: ____ Term: ____

Student loans

_____ Principal: ____ Monthly payment ____ Rate: ____ Term: ____

_____ Principal: ____ Monthly payment ____ Rate: ____ Term: ____

_____ Principal: ____ Monthly payment ____ Rate: ____ Term: ____

Car loan/lease payments

_____ Principal: ____ Monthly payment ____ Rate: ____ Term: ____

_____ Principal: ____ Monthly payment ____ Rate: ____ Term: ____

_____ Principal: ____ Monthly payment ____ Rate: ____ Term: ____

Personal loans

_____ Principal: ____ Monthly payment ____ Rate: ____ Term: ____

_____ Principal: ____ Monthly payment ____ Rate: ____ Term: ____

Mortgages

_____ Principal: ____ Monthly payment ____ Rate: ____ Term: ____

_____ Principal: ____ Monthly payment ____ Rate: ____ Term: ____

Other

	Principal: ___ Monthly payment ___ Rate: ___ Term: ___
_____	Principal: ___ Monthly payment ___ Rate: ___ Term: ___
_____	Principal: ___ Monthly payment ___ Rate: ___ Term: ___
_____	Principal: ___ Monthly payment ___ Rate: ___ Term: ___

Total debt: _____

If you currently have loans and credit card debt, write the steps you plan to take to reduce and repay these debts.

_____

_____

_____

_____

_____

EXPERIMENT: ECONOMIZING STRATEGIES

Indicate which of the economizing strategies explored in this chapter would have the most impact on your current financial situation and quest to be a good steward of resources.

→ Choose smaller.

→ Make or do it yourself.

→ Fix or repair it.

→ Plan ahead.

→ Wait to buy and buy on sale.

→ Buy used.

→ Trade, borrow and share.

→ Enjoy what's free.

→ Scavenge and reuse.

→ Negotiate on price.

→ Buy quality.

→   Beware of the dark side.

→   Spend where it counts.

List three new economizing steps you plan to try.

_____

_____

_____

7

Live Generously and Spend Wisely

Command those who are rich in this present world not to be arrogant nor to put their hope in wealth, which is so uncertain, but to put their hope in God, who richly provides us with everything for our enjoyment. Command them to do good, to be rich in good deeds, and to be generous and willing to share. In this way they will lay up treasure for themselves as a firm foundation for the coming age, so that they may take hold of the life that is truly life.

1 TIMOTHY 6:17-19

Over the course of this book we've invited you to order your inner life by taking steps to name what matters most to you, to practice gratitude and trust, and to believe you have enough by embracing voluntary limits. And we've invited you to order your outer life by taking practical steps to value and align your time, create a spending plan, and maximize your resources. One result of working with these steps over a period of months or years is that you will be increasingly free to spend your time the way you choose, and possibly have more money than you need for immediate expenses. So the question becomes what to do with the freedom you achieve. In this chapter we'll look toward the future, exploring how you can give generously, spend consciously, invest wisely and choose meaningful work and service.

**Talking to Your Kids
About Wealth and Money**
Lisa Scandrette

When Hailey was five, she asked if a certain friend's family was poor. I was puzzled because in fact this child's family was fairly well-off. When I asked her why she was asking, Hailey explained, "Well, both of Zoe's parents work and you get to stay home with us. Are we rich?" At the time we had very little money, but I realized that how I answered would help form Hailey's view of money and abundance. So I said, "Yes, we are. We have everything we need, we have people who love us, and we are well cared for. We are very rich." Of course, I explained that her friend's parents had simply chosen another way to do things and that they too were rich in the same way that we were. But that conversation prompted me to think more deeply about how I can choose to see wealth and how I can communicate that view to our children. Our children absorb and inherit the scripts we live by. If we believe that we have enough and that we are abundantly cared for, our kids will also. The work you do now to cultivate gratitude, contentment and generosity will benefit your kids in the future.

THE RESPONSIBILITY OF WEALTH

By global standards, most of us are already well-off, if not wealthy. We don't have to think about whether we will have food to eat or a place to sleep, and most of us can, to a certain extent, choose where we will live, the kind of work we do, and how we want to spend our discretionary income. Our wealth is hard for us to recognize because nearly everyone we know is at least as well-off or relatively as well-off as we are. We tend to compare ourselves with those who are more well-off rather than with people who are less financially fortunate than we are. Acknowledging the abundance we have can help us gain a perspective that empowers us to live generously.

How does your yearly income compare with others around the world? In 2005 the global median income was $1,225, which means that half of the world's population lived on less than $1,225 a year. Eighty percent of the world's population lives on $10 a day or less ($3,650 a year). According to the most recent data provided by the World Bank, it only takes $34,000 a year in individual income after taxes to be among the richest 1 percent in the world. This means that even the poorest 5 percent of Americans are better off than two-thirds of the global population.[1] These calculations are figured by economists using purchasing power parity (PPP), adjusting for differences in currency and cost of living.[2]

Where do you estimate you rank in terms of global wealth?

How does this knowledge affect your perception of whether you have enough?

What can those of us with the most wealth do to care for and share with those who have less?

Even if you don't consider yourself wealthy at this moment, there is a good chance that at some point in your life you will have far more than you need. So the question becomes, What do we do with this increasing prosperity? Give it away? Retire early? Upgrade to a larger house or a more expensive lifestyle? Use our wealth to make more money? According to the collective wisdom of the Judeo-Christian

---

[1]Annalyn Censky, "Americans Make Up Half of the World's Richest 1%," *CNN.com,* January 4, 2012, http://money.cnn.com/2012/01/04/news/economy/world_richest/index.htm.

[2]Ruth Alexander, "Where Are You on the Global Pay Scale?" BBC News, March 29, 2012, www.bbc.co.uk/news/magazine-17512040.

Scriptures, wealth is given, not only to enjoy, but to bless others with and to do good. With wealth comes responsibility. As the early church father John Chrysostom wrote,

> So what is the skill that rich people should acquire? . . . They must learn how to use their wealth well, to the good of all the people around them. The ordinary craftsperson may think that that is an easy skill to learn. On the contrary, it is the hardest skill of all. It requires both great wisdom and great moral strength. Look at how many rich people fail to acquire it, and how few practice it to perfection.[3]

At some point in life many of us will reach financial sustainability: when the major expenses of life are behind us (home purchase, child raising, education, old-age preparation) and our predictable earning from work and passive income investments is more than we need to cover basic expenses. Typically the more we have, the more we spend on ourselves. To address this tendency, some people adopt a graduated tithe by increasing their charitable giving by 1 percent a year. Others find it helpful to decide on an amount of income they need to live sustainably and then commit to give away the rest. And others simply choose to earn only as much as they need, giving their time and skills to serve others without pay.

> *If you adopt a posture of radical contentment, how much do you estimate you would need to live sustainably through the end of your life?*
>
> *If you reach a point of financial sustainability, which posture of giving would be most attractive to you?*
> - *Adopting a graduated tithe*
> - *Giving away everything beyond a certain amount*
> - *Choosing to earn only what is needed and sharing time and skills without pay*

---

[3]John Chrysostom, "Four Discourses on the Parable of the Rich Young Man."

Start Now with What You Have
Lisa Scandrette

Hospitality is an art of generosity. We welcome another person as though that person were Jesus. It is creating a space of welcome and vulnerability between two people, an environment where love is embodied and the worth of the guest is affirmed. Hospitality intentionally welcomes the stranger, the other, the hard to love, while graciously meeting their needs.

Practicing hospitality can be challenging. Our schedules are full. Welcoming another requires time, and opportunities to show care often come spontaneously. We need to create more room in our schedules—leave margin where the unexpected can be accommodated without overwhelming us.

We can rethink how we offer ourselves to others. A guest can join us as we make dinner, take the kids to the park or to their activities. It helps me to slow my mind down and ask, How can I be present to this person, care for them and make room for them in my day?

People have told me, "I would practice hospitality if I had a bigger house" or "I would show more hospitality if I had more money." If we are unwilling to share our time, belongings or self when we have little, however, it is doubtful that we will share when we have much.

Abundance is not necessary for hospitality. In our little flat (1,200 square feet and one bathroom for the five of us), we often have overnight guests. Sometimes, the kids will move into one room and offer the guest their bedroom. Sometimes our guest has slept on our couch, and sometimes we have shared our room with another family or couple. We have enjoyed getting to know many interesting people as they stay in our home. We have enjoyed sharing food, both simple and more extravagant, with one another.

HOLDING WEALTH LOOSELY

When we asked Jack and Lori if we could interview them for this book, they hesitantly agreed. "I'm not sure how much progress we've made toward simplicity," Lori says, "but we have tried to be intentional about our choices." Lori, whose family's business brought her a significant inheritance as a young adult, had to choose early about how to live with wealth. Watching her parents she observed that even after the company was sold at a large profit they maintained a sensible, modest lifestyle. To this day they drive an older car and Lori's mom shops the clearance racks. "I wrestle with what it means for me to pursue simplicity when there's nothing I want that I can't afford," Lori says. "I don't know the stress of not having enough."

Jack's family also has wealth, making it even more important for both of them to be thoughtful about their lifestyle choices. "After Lori and I got married," Jack says, "we had to think through what good values to take from our families and the ways we wanted to live life and use our resources differently." They both chose work in local nonprofits serving homeless youth, women and children. Jack and Lori also made a conscious choice to live in a modest house in the city at a time when many people in their circumstances moved to more spacious homes in the suburbs. "We decided to orient our lives around family and relationships and to stay in the city, where our faith community grounded us." Jack and Lori often invite friends to live with them and love to use their home as a place of hospitality. "One of the best choices we've made is to surround ourselves with people we care for and respect, regardless of their financial situation," Lori adds. "We didn't want to raise our kids surrounded by wealth because we thought the pressures and expectations of exclusive private schools and vacation resorts would shape them in unhealthy ways."

There have been a few times when Jack and Lori have made decisions that they later realized didn't align with their deeper values. Early in their parenting they wondered what family life should look like and ended up reverting to what was known from their own experience.

When their children were very small, they bought a large house in an exclusive neighborhood. "The weeks after we bought it I couldn't sleep," says Jack. Their unrest continued to grow until they sold the home ten years later. "It was great to have a house where we could throw a party for a hundred people and have twenty-five people hanging out in the kitchen," Jack says, "but ultimately we decided that the time and money required for upkeep didn't fit our values and who we want to be." They've since moved to a smaller house in a more modest neighborhood.

Once, Jack took a job that required more time and travel, which made them feel disconnected as a family. At the nonprofit where he had previously worked, the whole family knew the staff and supported the mission. "That helped me realize that one of my values is choosing work that can incorporate my family. Growing up, work, money and financial security often came at the expense of family relationships," Jack says. He left that job and found one more consistent with the values that he and Lori wanted to prioritize.

Jack and Lori have also made thoughtful choices about their spending and charitable giving. Rather than giving to the symphony or their alma maters, they prefer to support organizations and causes they are personally involved with where their giving can have a deeper impact. While much of their charitable giving goes toward addressing issues of poverty and justice, they also recognize that beauty and aesthetics are important to human thriving. "We love to travel and experience new cultures and support local artists and artisans," Jack adds. "As with everything, it's a balance. We deeply appreciate the money that big philanthropists give toward civic projects, because everyone benefits from the arts and education they make possible. For us, it resonates more to give where we can also invest ourselves. Giving for us might include donating to an organization we know and trust, supporting someone's craft or participating in amazing cultural events. It's all part of coming under people, helping them take strong steps toward who they want to be and contributing to work that makes the world a better place."

They also love to share what they have with friends. In Lori's family of origin, homes and possessions were sometimes shared, but with reservation. "We think, what's real stewardship? Why invest in a vacation home or a great vehicle if you can't share it with others or it alienates people? How can our possessions be part of how we share life with others? We try to avoid being weighed down by what we have and free to share what we own liberally." Although they try to be sensible about spending, they also see the value of throwing a great party, doing their best to assure that people of many backgrounds feel welcome. "Life is quite simply more fun if you don't hold on too tightly," they said.

"Of course, knowing that our choices matter, the food we eat is a huge reflection of our values, so we try to eat locally, sustainably, fairly and in ways that support people well. Making ethical choices about feeding family and friends is complicated and even tiring at times," says Lori. "We learn a lot from others in these areas."

Jack and Lori realize that many of the choices they are free to make come from their privileged First World context. "The teachings of Jesus about poverty and wealth are so compelling," Lori says. "We don't ever want to be settled or comfortable with our understanding of those teachings. We believe we're called to stay in the struggle." Jack concludes, "We are incredibly blessed. We have what we have, and there's no value in pretending otherwise. We think it's important for us to live in the creative tension of what it looks like for us to align our resources with our faith and values. It's a continuing journey."

GIVE GENEROUSLY

During her Nobel Peace Prize acceptance speech in 1979, Mother Teresa said, "The spiritual poverty of the West is harder to overcome than the hunger of the poor in India."[4] The deceitfulness of wealth can blind us to the true substance of life, and the truth that it is more blessed to give than to receive (Acts 20:35). In a well-known passage from the book of Isaiah the prophet addresses a group of people des-

---

[4]Dan Wooding, "The Day Mother Teresa Told Me, 'Your Poverty Is Greater Than Ours,'" *AssistNews.net*, July 4, 2010, www.assistnews.net/Stories/2010/s10070019.htm.

perate to experience divine intimacy. They had been observing a day of fasting, praying that God would come near to heal their souls. In response to what he observed, the prophet spoke:

> Is not this the kind of fasting I have chosen:
> to loose the chains of injustice
>   and untie the cords of the yoke,
> to set the oppressed free
>   and break every yoke?
> Is it not to share your food with the hungry
>   and to provide the poor wanderer with shelter—
> when you see the naked, to clothe them,
>   and not to turn away from your own flesh and blood?
> (Isaiah 58:6-7)

Isaiah promised that if the people spent themselves "in behalf the hungry [to] satisfy the needs of the oppressed," that their healing would "quickly appear" (Isaiah 58:10, 8). We often think it is the poor who need healing, when actually it may be us as well. In the great parable of the sheep and the goats, Jesus echoes this invitation to live in wholeness by caring for those who are hungry, thirsty, naked, sick and lonely, saying, "Whatever you did for one of the least of these brothers and sisters of mine, you did for me" (Matthew 25:40).

Our friend Rick Slone, who serves the homeless in Salinas, California, says that there are two places where God's presence is sure to be found: in the stillness of prayer and in the company of those who struggle and suffer—because God's heart is always with the poor. As Tolstoy observed, "Where love is, God is."[5]

BECOME A FRIEND TO THE POOR

We can take steps to live generously by becoming a friend to the poor, beginning with the people closest to us who might be struggling. Vis-

---

[5]Leo Tolstoy, "Where Love Is, God Is," Holy Trinity, New Rochelle, accessed December 11, 2012, www.holytrinitynewrochelle.org/tolstoychristmas.html.

iting a soup kitchen or volunteering at a nursing home are good first steps. Over the past couple of years we've volunteered at a food pantry which has allowed us to know neighbors we wouldn't have met otherwise who struggle with family difficulties, mental health issues or chemical dependency. Many of our neighbors have lost relatives to gang violence and often wear T-shirts featuring a photo of their slain uncle, cousin or son. Being involved at the food pantry helps us put our stresses and concerns into perspective and reminds us of what is most basic, cherished and important—love, safety, relationships and food shared among family, friends and neighbors.

If you ever get a chance, you may want to cross international boundaries to get a broader perspective on issues of global need. Several years ago I traveled with our daughter Hailey to El Salvador, where we visited rural families and development sites. We were particularly interested in El Salvador since many of our neighbors are refugees of its civil war of the 1980s. Our neighborhood is decorated with murals commemorating the life of civil rights leader Archbishop Oscar Romero, who was assassinated for his outspoken support of human rights in El Salvador.

At a church school site in the Santa Ana region we met Yahaira, a pretty five-year-old girl. The children at the center seemed so happy and clean that at first it was hard to believe this was a center dedicated to helping families in dire need. After touring the center, Yahaira took Hailey's hand and led us past the local Toyota dealership, where we took a left turn down a dirt road. That's where things began to look very different. The road was lined with small shanties, guarded by dogs and makeshift security fences. Yahaira led us across a stream, filthy with motor oil, garbage and old paint cans, to her "house"—a few boards built into one room shared by eight family members. The stream we crossed was the family's only water supply. I was told by a development worker that if I drank its water, it would make me very sick or possibly kill me, but Yahaira and her family had developed immunity to this poisoned water over many years. While I talked with Yahaira's mother, Hailey played with Yahaira. I learned that the family survives on $2 a day. Knowing that the dollar sets the market in that country, food costs are relatively the same as those in the US. I tried to imagine how eight people could eat nutritionally on a quarter per person per day. Their diet consists mostly of handmade corn meal tortillas and a few cooked beans. We decided to sponsor Yahaira through a development organization, which provides her with nutritious food, access to health care, education and spiritual guidance. Before we left, we stood in the shack, holding hands as Yahaira's mother led us in prayer, thanking God for everything provided to us. Rarely a day goes by when I don't think about Yahaira and her family, and question my impulse for a second cup of coffee or a three-dollar treat. The often observed irony is that perhaps we need the poor more than the poor need us, to teach us how to live gratefully.

You may want to consider how to give a portion of your resources to help the poorest people in the world. Organizations like Compassion International and World Vision specialize in helping people develop local solutions to issues of poverty, hunger, sanitation and clean water. Sometimes, efforts to help can actually hurt, so you'll want to do some research to determine what kind of development support is most effective and empowering.

> *What is a next step you want to take to serve those who are hungry, thirsty, naked, sick, lonely or in prison in your city or region?*
>
> *What issues of global need and development are you most passionate about? What organizations are working to address those issues that you could support with your time, talents and money?*

SPEND CONSCIOUSLY

While waiting at the San Salvador airport to board our plane back to the United States I bought two pounds of roasted coffee. Later I discovered that much of the arable land in El Salvador is used to cultivate coffee beans, the majority of which are exported to the United States and Europe. So a country that struggles to feed its own people is leveraging its land in order to compete in the global economy, often paying workers extremely low wages and treating the land poorly. We are challenged to become more aware of how our spending makes a real difference in the lives of people both locally and globally. Getting our luxury items at the cheapest price comes at a significant cost to our migrant neighbors or people in the Two-Thirds World. Many have observed the connection between low-cost commodities, like coffee, chocolate and textiles, and the global slave trade, including children forced to work long hours for exceptionally low wages. To address this concern some coffee importers to the United States arrange for direct trade with El Salvadorian fincas (farms) at higher prices to ensure fair wages, good working conditions and ecologically sustainable farming practices.

One of the ways we can do good with our wealth is to vote with our spending. We can voluntarily choose to spend more for items that are made ethically and sustainably, including meats, fruits and vegetables, and other goods that are certified as fairly traded and slavery free. How much would you have to pay for a shirt that was made fairly? Probably three or four times what it might cost at a national clothing store chain. These kinds of choices will increase our expenses, but as many have observed, the high cost of cheap goods is currently being paid by migrant workers and those living in the Two-Thirds World.

The principle of voting with your spending extends to a wide range of issues and concerns. The practice of frugality can be balanced by understanding the reality of commerce and a commitment to paying a fair price for what we value. Whatever we fund with our dollars will persist in the future. If you like local shops in your neighborhood, then they need your business. If you enjoy hearing local musicians, you can be a patron of their craft by paying for their music and performances. If you value new ideas and creative expressions, you can support the work of writers or artists you believe in by buying their creations. If we appreciate the contribution of an innovative organization or faith expression, those groups need our dollars to stay in existence. Many people also apply this principle to their banking and investing, choosing to put their assets into green and ethical invest-

Why Consider Locally Grown Food?

- *Each food item in a typical American meal has traveled 1,500 miles in the course of its life. If each family were to eat just one meal a week comprising locally and organically raised meats and produce, we would reduce our country's oil consumption by 1.1 million barrels of oil every week.[a]*

- *When produce is purchased at the grocery store, farmers receive eighteen cents for every dollar. Middlemen get the rest.[b]*

- *Food purchased from the farmer is fresh! It was picked ripe and has more nutrients and taste.*

- *A diversity of crops is better and important. Most commercial food is bred to be durable for shipping, but there are regional heirloom varieties of vegetables that differ in taste, texture and resistance to disease. Many question the wisdom of losing all the old seed varieties—what happens if a pest or disease attacks one of the main commercial varieties?*

- *Farmers in developing countries who produce foods for us are often not paid well, and the crop diversity in their own countries suffers while the middlemen get rich off their cheap labor and global competition. They would be better off selling within their country and so would their own people. Global food trade often makes the economy of developing countries outstrip the ability of the citizens of that country to buy the food that they produce.*

---

[a]See Barbara Kingsolver with Steven L. Hopp and Camille Kingsolver, *Animal, Vegetable, Miracle: A Year of Food Life* (New York: Harper Perennial, 2008).
[b]See Cathleen Hockman-Wert and Mary Beth Lind, *Simply in Season*, 2nd ed. (Scottdale, PA: Herald Press, 2009).

ments that do not fund war machinery and instead support emerging economies. A rather peculiar saying of Jesus is, "Use worldly wealth to gain friends for yourselves, so that when it is gone, you will be welcomed into eternal dwellings" (Luke 16:9). By spending consciously we make friends and participate in economic development.

> *What are the votes you want to cast through your purchasing practices?*

INVEST WISELY

In the well-known parable of the talents Jesus tells a story about a landowner who went on a long journey, leaving each of his servants with a certain amount of money to manage. Two of his servants invested the funds and soon doubled their money. The third servant went out, dug a hole and buried the cash because he was afraid to take a risk. When the master returned he praised the first two servants but was furious with the third, saying, "That's a terrible way to live! It's criminal to live cautiously like that! If you knew I was after the best, why did you do less than the least? The least you could have done would have been to invest the sum with the bankers, where at least I would have gotten a little interest" (Matthew 25:26-27 *The Message*). Through this passage Jesus seems to suggest that we've got to take risks to be good stewards of what we've been given—perhaps not just with money but also with our time and talents. Money can be spent, it can be saved, or it can be invested to make more money. For long-term sustainability and financial freedom, saving will only get us so far, but if we learn to invest wisely we can create passive income so that we are less dependent on earnings from a job or paid work. Over the long term, we will also have more to give. To multiply resources, some people invest in the stock market or mutual funds. Others invest in rental property or a small business venture. Managing tenants or trading stocks is fun for some people and incredibly stressful for others. You have to do your homework and decide what level of involvement and risk you are comfortable with. A good first step, if you haven't done so already, is to purchase an asset, like a home that you can either live in or rent out. Investments should not be confused with get-rich-quick schemes. Gathering money little by little is a safer and wiser way to build assets (Proverbs 12:12). And it's best to invest in multiple ventures, since you don't know which investments will turn out well and which will perform poorly (Ecclesiastes 11:2).

Are you excited or hesitant about taking risks to invest your resources? Explain.

What kind of investing seems like the best fit for you?

Retirement

In our culture retirement is often associated with cruise ship vacations and leisurely days spent on the golf course. This picture of the years after paid employment are over assumes retirement as a reward, a time to live it up after years slogging away at a tedious job. But if you've chosen to live purposefully from your deeper values, why would you want to retire? Research suggests that seeing retirement as the end of a life of responsibility is actually bad for our health.[c] We need a purpose beyond ourselves. If we have planned well for years of less earning, we can be free to give our time to what we feel most passionate about, and we can live generously and leave a financial legacy.

[c]"Early Retirement: Bad For Your Health?" *Freakonomics*, March 29, 2012, www.freakonomics.com/2012/03/29/early-retirement-bad-for-your-health.

CHOOSE MEANINGFUL WORK AND SERVICE

One of the greatest assets we have is our ability to work and serve. We've been given time, talents and skills that can be used to seek the greater good. If our time is our life, then the work we choose to do can be an important reflection of our deeper values.

A few years ago I was talking with a young man who came to me for spiritual direction. During our conversation he happened to mention the amount of his yearly salary. "Wow," I blurted, "that's way more than I make and I'm ten years older than you." Without hesitation he quickly replied, "Yes, but you do what you love. I give the best hours of my week to fund someone else's agenda."

With paid work we give our time, talents and skills in exchange for money, power or prestige. In developed countries, most of us are not driven in our work by sheer necessities like food, clothing and shelter. If we were, most of us would hardly have to work. Our motives for work are much more complex. John grew up in a poor family; there often wasn't enough and he felt deprived. He's driven in his career by a desire to have more comfort and security. Anthony never went to college and makes a lot of money to prove that he is smart. Jane strives to be successful as a patent attorney in order to meet the expectations of her immigrant parents who sacrificed so much to give her opportunities. Inspired by reformers like Cesar Chavez and Martin Luther King Jr., Carlos wants to make a difference in the lives of new immigrants.

There are a variety of reasons we choose our work. Which of the following statements best describes your motive?

+ My work pays what I need and provides comfort and security.

+ My work gives me an important status or role.

+ My work utilizes my gifts and talents.

+ My work embodies my deeper goals and passions.

We're not saying that any of these motives are necessarily better than another. But knowing what drives your work decisions can help you see what your tradeoffs are. Your job may give you the comfort and security you want, but leave you longing for deeper significance. Or the responsibility of a high-status job may be fulfilling but leave you feeling stressed and having less energy for the rest of life. Choosing a job with significance can often, though not always, mean lower pay. There isn't always a clear tradeoff between meaningful work and financial success, yet any path you choose will have its limitations, challenges and opportunities. When we are conscious of those tradeoffs we can make better decisions about our work choices.

Taking steps to simplify can give you more freedom to choose the kind of work you do.

After ten years working as a global business consultant, Selina had a growing passion for the well-being of women in the Two-Thirds World. She decided to take a much lower paying job as the development director of an organization that offers microloans to women. Selina willingly traded her high-status job for work that utilizes her gifts and aligns with her passions.

When I first moved to the inner-city neighborhood where we live, when I met someone I would typically ask, "What do you do?" (meaning, "What is your job?"). Some of my neighbors were hesitant to answer—because they were either unemployed or what they did to earn a living was technically illegal. Other neighbors wouldn't answer my question but instead would say, "I'm an artist" or "I'm a musician." I would probe a bit, trying to figure out whether they were successfully earning a living as an artist or musician. Often they weren't and worked on the side as a taxi driver, bartender or accountant. By evading my question, they were telling me that they didn't want to be defined by how they made money but by what they were passionate about. I learned something from that, and ever since I make a habit of asking, "How do you spend your time?" rather than "What do you do?"

How closely connected are your work and your sense of identity?

The shift from an agrarian to a postindustrial society, all in the span of less than one hundred years, has radically redefined our understanding of work and identity. A hundred years ago, 80 percent of Americans made their living as small, independent farmers. Today, less than 2 percent of us are involved in agricultural work. Civic and social life were previously built on household economies in which family members together provided for their material needs through the labor of their hands, which was supplemented by trade, bartering and cash exchange. It's fair to say that most people had a more integrated existence, with a sense of place, physical labor and relationships intersecting at many points every day.

While most of us would prefer not to go back to long hours of manual labor and dependence on volatile weather patterns, the shift to a postindustrial age has had several unintended consequences that we must now grapple with. Most of us view our work in terms of what we are paid, rather than for what our work directly produces to provide for our families and communities. We primarily use currency to buy what we need or want. Few of us own the means of production (e.g., land, tools or a business), so when we conceive of livelihood we think of a paycheck rather than assets. Our income-producing work is often disconnected from our neighborhoods and families. This has reinforced our tendency to see ourselves as individual wage earners rather than members of a household or village economy. When work feels disconnected from life, we tend to "live for the weekends," seeking escape from the meaninglessness and isolation of our jobs through endless entertainments.

As a culture we are grappling with how to renew a sense of place, family and village, and participation in a local economy. But to accomplish this we'll have to learn to think and behave differently and consider tradeoffs between money and meaning that might lead to a more satisfying and sustainable lifestyle. A movement of creative dreamers and social entrepreneurs are pioneering new ways to integrate work with life for the greater good. Pursing simplicity with time and money allows the freedom to experiment with a new understanding of livelihood, seeing both paid and unpaid work as the expression of one's calling or vocation, rather than merely a job and a paycheck.

Do you find your present work meaningful? Does it take you out of your neighborhood and community or bring you closer to a sense of common good?

Our friends Darin and Meeghan Petersen have sought to live creatively, believing that if they follow their passions their needs will be provided for. When they were in their early twenties they started a church community and a nonprofit that served the needs of the marginalized. While they did this, Meeghan worked as a social worker, and Darin earned a small stipend from the organization. But they also bought a house, and with the help of roommates paid it off in four years. During that same time period they bought five other housing units, not primarily to earn passive income but to help redevelop their neighborhood and to provide good, safe housing to working poor families.

Having assets and few fixed expenses provided them with the freedom to make decisions and take on projects based on passions rather than financial considerations. They invited an elderly friend with Alzheimer's to be a part of their family. They traveled the world and lived in several countries making friends and doing development work, eventually to one location to raise their two boys.

Darin now divides his time between directing an organization called The Simple Way, developing a nonprofit redistribution website called Common Change and providing private consulting to various organizations and individuals. Each of these projects, along with their real estate investments, provides a modest stream of income. They've made a conscious decision to set their income limit at $25,000 a year, plus the cost of their housing in whatever city they are currently living in. Darin says, "We seek to be generous and responsible. I have a full life, but everything I do has a purpose, fuels my passions and gives me an opportunity to utilize my gifts." When I asked Darin why more people don't make choices that allow them to be free with their time and money, he said, "A lot of us settle. We stop taking risks and give up on our dreams. I don't ever want to settle."

As you look toward a future of greater freedom, what are the dreams and new risks you would like to take to live generously and spend wisely? Consider your next steps in the following areas:

BEING A FRIEND TO THE POOR

- ☐ Find a way to connect and become a better friend to the poor in your city or region.
- ☐ Contribute toward global needs through a responsible development organization.
- ☐ Adopt a graduated tithe by increasing what you give by 1 percent a year.
- ☐ Decide on an amount of income you need and give away the rest.
- ☐ Choose to earn only as much as you need, and give your time and work to serve without pay.
- ☐ Other: _____
- ☐ Other: _____

SPEND CONSCIOUSLY

How would you like to spend more consciously to cast your vote about the world you want to live in?

- ☐ Research and adopt fair trade, slavery free and ecologically sustainable purchasing practices.
- ☐ Make purchases that support businesses and products that you believe in.
- ☐ Support artists, writers, artisans and organizations whose work you appreciate.
- ☐ Spend to make friends and offer hospitality.
- ☐ Other: _____

☐ Other: _____

CHOOSE MEANINGFUL WORK AND SERVICE

☐ Consciously embrace how my current work allows me to do good and utilize use my gifts.

☐ Transition to work that is more closely aligned with my gifts and deeper passions.

☐ Work less so that I can devote more of my time to other passions and volunteer service.

☐ Explore options for multiple streams of passive income to have more flexibility and time to pursue my passions.

☐ Rekindle a sense of the "household economy" by making and trading goods and services.

☐ Other: _____

☐ Other: _____

INVEST WISELY

☐ Purchase assets that can provide income in the future (property, a business or further education).

☐ Transition banked assets and investments to ethical and green institutions.

☐ Intentionally invest in companies that create jobs in emerging markets and support ethical and sustainable global development.

☐ Other: _____

☐ Other: _____

Conclusion

We wrote this book with the hope and confidence that we can each take steps to become more free to spend our time and money on what matters most. This confidence is inspired by three core beliefs:

→ We were created with the purpose to seek the greater good of God's kingdom.

→ We have enough.

→ We can make intentional choices about how we spend our time and money.

Through the exercises, tasks and experiments of each chapter we've invited you to

1. Name what matters most to you.

2. Value and align your time.

3. Practice gratitude and trust.

4. Believe you have enough by embracing voluntary limits.

5. Create a spending plan.

6. Maximize your resources.

7. Live generously and spend wisely.

As you've worked through these steps, some may have been easier or more fun than others. With certain steps you might have encountered resistance or noted an area you would like to revisit and work on more. We don't think this is a one-time process. Most of us experience change gradually and in layers over months and years, or we come to a deeper level of understanding in new stages of life. Keep working with the steps that make sense to you and take another step when you feel ready. You may find it helpful to review these steps at least once a year. As a way to reflect on your process, we recommend completing the simplicity self-evaluation on page 124.

Experiencing a life of simplicity and freedom is an ongoing process that sometimes involves a sense of frustration or failure. Maybe you struggle to stick with your spending plan or find yourself falling back into patterns of worry or consumption. We can learn from our failed attempts to live in gratitude, trust, contentment and generosity. Our struggles and resistance to simplicity may reveal deeper levels of disordered attachment. This awareness can propel us to seek greater healing through further soul work. God always invites us to a life that is freer and lighter than the false paths we create for ourselves (Matthew 11:28-29).

The invitation of simplicity allows us to make space for life to grow—bearing the fruit of love in our lives. We believe that community is vital to this process. A group of supportive friends who share your commitment to simplicity can help you take steps or make changes that would be difficult on your own. Together you can create a local culture of sharing, generosity and conscious living. Simplicity, for instance, is one of the core commitments of our faith community in San Francisco, and once a year we work through many of the steps in this book together.

If you completed the tasks in each chapter, you have a packet of information, a simplicity plan, that you can review and reference to stay on track with your progress. We suggest that you use this packet to review and update your goals and spending plan at least once a year, if not once a quarter.

We would love to know how working through the steps in this book has been helpful to you. You can contact us at info@reimagine.org.

May you be free to spend your time and money on what matters most!

The universe produces all that is needed:
Food and Fabrics,
Water and Wood,
Bricks and Clay,
Sunshine and Rain.
The Maker brings these to us as a gift each day
—knowing that we are happiest
when we live close to the soil
aware of our source
consciously embracing all things with thanks.

The secret is that we are fabulously wealthy
Living like Kings and Queens
In a garden of leisure and luxury.
What we have is enough . . . and more
If we lack anything, it is the simple pleasure
To enjoy what we already possess
Though so often we find ourselves
chasing after joyless schemes and business
denying our inheritance
And wanting what can only make us choked, tired and desperate.

Today, let us find goodness
In the small things
Tasting the abundance you have lavished on us
With eager open hands
Giving and receiving
Trusting and Completing
the circle that began
With the gift of life.[1]

---

[1]Previously published in Mark Scandrette, *Practicing the Way of Jesus* (Downers Grove, IL: InterVarsity Press, 2011), p. 139.

Acknowledgments

*T*hanks to our friend Damon Snyder who partnered with us to develop the original ReImagine Simplicity workshop from which this project originated. And thanks to many friends who allowed us to share your stories and interviews in these pages.

Thanks to the many people who have participated in our Simplicity Workshops and Simplify Learning Labs over the years. Your courage to risk and experiment together helped inspire and equip us to bring these insights and practices to a wider audience. We are also gratefully indebted to the many patrons of ReImagine who have believed in and supported the work of our organization through the years.

Conversations at Mission Pie with Rosa Lee Harden and Jarrod Shappell were significant to the development of this book.

The following early readers worked through the material with their communities and provided valuable feedback: Theresa Parks, Heather Newman Hahn, Ben Yosua-Davis, Marianne Kesler, Jessie Krohn and Jenni Joy. Ben Younan's insightful comments on the draft manuscript shaped and significantly improved the finished product. Thanks also to Amber Younan and the money group at Solomon's Porch for being an offsite pilot for the small group guide.

We are grateful for a happy partnership with Intervarsity Press, including Dave Zimmerman, Andrew Bronson, Nathan Baker-Lutz and Adrianna Wright.

We are glad to have shared this journey and long-term experiment in simplicity with our children, Hailey, Noah and Isaiah. Special thanks to Hailey for sidebar contributions.

Group Learning Guide

W*orking through the steps in this book* with a group of people can provide the solidarity and support needed for lasting change and can create a profound sense of community and trust among participants. Here are a few tips for initiating and leading a group, adapted from my book *Practicing the Way of Jesus*.

1. *Form a team of two to three people who will initiate the learning group and facilitate sessions.* We can't stress enough how important and helpful it can be to have collaborators in this process. When you collaborate you have a greater pool of skills and wisdom to draw from, and a wider network of potential participants to invite.

You will want to decide together when and where you will meet, how you will invite participants and the roles each person will play during your group sessions. People in your group will only be as invested and authentic as the facilitators are. The honesty, self-awareness and commitment to growth and change you model will set the tone for the entire group. Make sure your core team has the time and space necessary to facilitate this process.

2. *As you invite people into the learning group, make the opportunity and expectations for participation clear.* You are inviting participants into an intensive and practical process to become more free to spend time and money on what matters most. Working through the steps in this book together will be more of a learning journey than a book study. If you are introducing this opportunity to an existing group that meets for other purposes, you will want to emphasize the unique intensity and commitment to action this process will require. People will

get the most out of this experience by making a commitment to participate fully in the process by attending all sessions, reading the assigned chapter, and completing tasks and exercises before the next session. To solidify this commitment, invite participants to sign the group learning contract at your first session together (see below).

Here are a few things to keep in mind as you invite people to participate:

+ The main purpose of this eight-session intensive is to develop skills for taking practical steps to simplify by aligning life vision, values, time and financial practices.

+ For momentum and group safety it is important to attend each session. It is best not to allow new people into the group after the first week.

+ The time commitment required includes a one- to two-hour group meeting, one hour of reading, chapter exercises, experiments and tasks that will take fifteen to thirty minutes a day (or a two- to four-hour slot) before each session.

+ Don't be surprised if a few people decline your invitation or drop out partway through. It's common for 5-10 percent of a group to drop out of a high-intensity process like this in the first week or two.

3. Plan activities for the session ahead of time. The group learning guide includes ninety minutes of activities. Estimated times for specific session activities are provided but flexible; expect them to take slightly more or less time depending on the dynamics of your group. If possible, allow two hours to meet, including fifteen minutes of socializing before and after session activities. You can shorten your session to an hour by eliminating some of the suggested activities, but most groups who have gone through this process say they could always use more time for discussion.

Each session includes the following elements:

+ A welcome and opening prayer or reflection

+ Discussion of some aspect of the assigned chapter

→ A suggested Scripture to engage with as a group

→ A check-in on the exercises, tasks and experiments of the assigned chapter (done in smaller huddle groups of three to four people)

→ A group exercise that explores a theme from the chapter

→ A seven- to eight-minute video (available at www.ivpress.com/free-videos, using the access code fru8wef2)

→ A review of exercises, task and experiments to complete before the next session

→ A closing prayer

As you look at the guide for each session, decide what activities are most relevant to your group. There may be more suggested activities than you have time for.

4. Always include check-in and review what to do before the next session. These are important elements of the learning process, providing accountability and support for new steps of action. If there are more than five people in your group, we recommend dividing up into smaller "huddle" groups of three to four people to check in on exercises. You will want to have a designated facilitator for each huddle group. It can be helpful to set a time limit for sharing so that each person has an opportunity to share their thoughts and experiences.

5. Create a welcoming, conversational and supportive environment. Your willingness to risk honesty and transparency about your successes and failures will empower others to do the same. Try to include everyone in conversation. Invite less talkative people to respond to questions, and gently redirect over-talkers by saying something like, "Okay, now let's hear from someone who hasn't had a chance to share yet." Be creative and make your group experience fun, lively and unpredictable.

Many of the topics brought up in this process lead to emotional sharing. Be prepared to care for and walk alongside people as they face regrets, new realizations, and invitations to greater freedom and healing. Some people in your group may need more space to process outside of group sessions or assistance completing tasks and exercises.

6. *Think about who is in the room.* Consider the ages, life stages and circumstances of the people in your group. Choose activities and discussion topics that are relevant to the people in your circle. Not everyone has the same strengths or growth edges when it comes to this process. You may need to occasionally speak up for an under-represented perspective so that each participant's life experience is acknowledged.

7. *Regularly remind your group of the vision and goals of this process.* Some people will be taking courageous and challenging new steps in their lives. With the effort required, sometimes it's easy to forget the "why" for specific tasks or activities. The tasks and exercises for each session are designed to help participants live in abundance, gratitude, contentment and generosity and experience the freedom to spend time and money on what matters most.

8. *Follow up your weekly session with an email to participants.* After each session send a note that summarizes the discussion, offers encouragement, and reminds people of the experiment and tasks the group committed to do before the next session.

9. *Near the end of your process invite the group to consider, "What's next?"* Walking through the steps in this book together can lead to a strong sense of community and trust. The group may want to consider ways to stay connected on a monthly or quarterly basis to keep on track with their commitments and steps to growth. Or the group may want to form a shared giving circle to live out a commitment to live generously (for more about this, visit commonchange.org).

10. *Consider extending the number of sessions from eight to twelve.* We've designed the steps in this book around eight sessions because we've found that after eight weeks group energy and momentum begin to wane. But if your group is willing to commit up front to a longer time frame, there are advantages to spending more time working through the exercises and tasks in each chapter.

USING *FREE* VIDEOS

Included with your purchase of *Free* is access to eight videos that have been developed to deepen the experience of a group committed to taking these steps together.

Each video is a bridge between chapters that gives your group a chance to discuss how they experienced the previous chapter. As a group you will commit to completing exercises, tasks and experiments in the next chapter and also the ones suggested in each video.

Before your first meeting, everyone in the group should read the introduction. During your first meeting, discuss what you read and your motivation for committing to this process together. Then watch Video One, discuss the content, and commit to the steps you'll take between meetings. Follow this pattern as your work through each chapter and video:

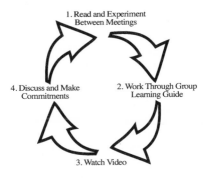

1. Read and Experiment Between Meetings
2. Work Through Group Learning Guide
3. Watch Video
4. Discuss and Make Commitments

Here are examples of what your group might discuss after you watch each video:

+ How does this story apply to us? What can we learn?

+ What do we struggle with in this part of the process? Where do we excel?

+ Which of the experiments are we going to commit to between meetings?

+ How can we support each other between meetings?

Group Learning Contract

Making a promise is a powerful way to stay motivated and accountable while you are taking steps to grow and change. Consider signing this learning contract as a group during your first session together.

I am committing myself to a process of becoming more free to spend my time and money on what matters most. I understand that this process involves taking my next steps to

1. name what matters most
2. value and align my time
3. practice gratitude and trust
4. believe I have enough
5. create a spending plan
6. maximize my resources
7. live generously and spend wisely

To effectively take my next steps in these areas, I will

* participate in all group sessions
* arrive on time to each meeting
* contact the group leader(s) ahead of time if I have to be absent due to unforeseen illness or a scheduling conflict
* read the assigned chapter and complete exercises, tasks and experiments before each session
* share openly and honestly with the group
* listen compassionately and keep what is shared in the group confidential
* enlist a friend from inside (or outside) the group to listen, encourage and support me during this process

Signature: _____ Date: _____

Name of the person I've asked to encourage and support me as I take these steps:

_____

A Prayer of Abundance

(for group use)

We know that we are cared for by an abundant Provider.
Let us choose to be grateful and trusting.

We know that we have enough and that what
we need will always be provided.
Let us choose to be content and generous.

We know that our choices matter for ourselves,
for others and for future generations.
*Help us to live consciously and creatively, celebrating the
signs of your New Creation that is present and coming.*

Creator, who made us to seek the greater good of your kingdom,
*Guide us to spend our time, talents and
resources on what matters most.*

Teach us to be free,
to live without worry, fear or greed in the freedom of your abundance.

Give us our daily bread, as we share ours with the hungry.
We give you thanks for the precious gift of life!

SESSION 1

Make Space for Life to Grow

Before the first session:

+ **Read** "Why We Wrote This Book," "How to Use This Book" and the introduction.

+ **Complete** the journal exercise "Your Money Story" on page 39. Come to the session prepared to share your story.

+ **Fill out** the "Time, Money and Meaning Self-Assessment" on page 40 and "Chart Your Direction of Change" on page 43.

Optional daily readings on themes from the book's opening section:

+ The parable of the sower (Luke 8:1-15)

+ Life rooted in its source (Psalm 1)

+ A flourishing life (Psalm 52)

+ Space and growth (Psalm 92)

+ In praise of a fruitful life (Psalm 128)

+ The Creator as source (John 15:1-17)

+ The fruits of a flourishing life (Galatians 5:13-26)

Goals for this session:

+ Help each other feel welcome and connected, and take steps to build trust.

+ Reflect on the invitation of Jesus into a flourishing life with space for growth and vitality.

+ Explore how you've been shaped by your "money story."

+ Value your strengths and reflect on where you would like to see change in your relationships with time, money, meaning, global equity and sustainability.

+ Review and sign contract of participation as a group.

WELCOME (5 minutes)

Each person should introduce themselves and answer the following questions: What made you interested in being part of this process? What do you hope to gain from this experience?

PRAYER (5 minutes)

Read "A Prayer of Abundance (for group use)" on page 227 aloud together.

Which line of the prayer do you most resonate with? Why?

Are there any statements in the prayer that you struggle to believe or that sound too good to be true? Explain.

DISCUSSION ON READINGS (10 minutes)

What thoughts or questions surfaced as you read the opening pages of this book?

What preconceived notions or "baggage" do you have about "simplicity" and "financial freedom"?

What do you hope will be different about the focus of this group?

What will help you stay open to the process?

SCRIPTURE (10 minutes)

Have someone in the group read the parable of the sower (Luke 8:1-14). Reflect together on how this passage speaks to the invitation to simplicity.

What is the picture of a flourishing life that Jesus describes?

"Life's worries, riches and pleasures." Which of these threats to flourishing do you most identify with? What holds you back from the free and flourishing life you were created for?

How would you like to be more fruitful and free with your time, talents and resources?

HUDDLE (5 minutes)

Divide into groups of three or four. Check in with each other on the "before session" exercises in "Why We Wrote This Book," "How to Use This Book" and "Making Space for Life to Grow."

MY MONEY STORY (25 minutes)

Take turns sharing a five-minute version of your "What's Your Money Story" journal exercise. After each person has shared, take a few moments as a group to reflect back what you heard in each story, offering words of support and encouragement.

STRENGTH AND GROWTH AREAS (5 minutes)

Review the "Time, Money and Meaning Self-Assessment" (p. 40) together.

What did you identify as your greatest area of strength? Why?

Work and Meaning   Time Management   Soul Issues

Money Management   Global Sustainability

Which of these did you identify as your greatest area for growth? Explain.

CHART YOUR DIRECTION FOR CHANGE (5 minutes)

Take turns responding to the following questions.

Do you tend to be more pragmatic or idealistic? Explain.

Which direction of growth will bring the most new freedom to your life? What do you need to lean into: greater vision, practical skills or both?

SESSION 1 VIDEO (10 minutes)

Reunite as a larger group. Watch and discuss the video for session one.

LEARNING CONTRACT (5 minutes)

Read, briefly discuss and then sign the learning contract (p. 226). Share contact information for interaction between sessions.

TO DO (5 minutes)

Review the steps each participant should take before the next session:

+ **Enlist** a friend (inside or outside this group) to support you as you work through the steps in this book.
+ **Read** chapter one of *Free*.
+ **Complete** the "Who Am I?" journal exercise on page 53 (15-30 minutes).
+ **Develop** five words and statements to describe your deeper purpose (15-30 minutes).
+ **Create** one-year goals in key life areas (1-2 hours).

CLOSE (5 minutes)

Read "A Prayer of Abundance (for group use)" once more together.

Optional Daily Readings Before the Next Session
- → The good mandate given to humans (Genesis 1:26-31)
- → Made for love and fruitfulness (John 15:1-17)
- → The greatest command(s) (Mark 12:28-31)
- → Embracing the life you've been given (Ecclesiastes 2:17-26)
- → Where the heart find its treasure (Matthew 6:19-24)
- → Meditation on impermanence (Psalm 90)
- → Living with the end in mind (Ecclesiastes 9:1-10)

SESSION 2

Name What Matters Most to You

Goals for this session:
- → Explore questions of meaning and purpose together.
- → Encourage one another to identify and voice core aspects of identity.
- → Support one another's efforts to establish one-year goals in key life areas.

PRAYER (5 minutes)
Read "A Prayer of Abundance (for group use)" on page 227 aloud together.

CHAPTER DISCUSSION (10 minutes)
What stood out to you from the readings and activities in chapter one? Why?

Which of these four questions did you find easiest and most challenging to consider? Explain.
- → What is my ultimate purpose?
- → Who am I?
- → What's right in front of me?
- → What will matter in the end?

Why do you think a book about the freedom of simplicity would begin with a chapter on life purpose?

SCRIPTURE (10 minutes)

The way Jesus responded when he was asked about the greatest command reveals something about what matters most. Have someone read Mark 12:28-34 aloud, then reflect as a group on how this passage speaks of the invitation to simplicity.

If what matters most is so obvious and simple, why is loving God and people often so difficult?

What prevents us from having love as the primary focus of our lives?

What do you think Jesus meant when he told the man in the story, "You are not far from the kingdom of God" (Mark 12:34)?

What do you think it looks like to love God and neighbor as yourself?

HUDDLE (45 minutes)

Divide into groups of two or three (preferably the same group as the previous session) to check in on the tasks and exercises of the week.

Discuss the "Who Am I?" journal exercise from page 53. What clues did you uncover about your true identity and deeper purpose?

When you responded to these questions, what stood out to you or surprised you?

What do you particularly celebrate and enjoy about the person you were made to be?

Share your work on creating a purpose statement (p. 56) with each other. What are the five words and statements you developed to describe your deeper purpose?

Do you have the space and freedom to live into this picture of who you are and what you were made for? Why or why not?

What did the process of developing one-year goals (p. 60) clarify or reveal for you?

Share one or two of your one-year goals for a particular life area and the action steps which accompany that goal.

WHAT WILL MATTER IN THE END? (10 minutes)

Reunite as a larger group. Spend three minutes individually drawing a picture of what you hope to look like and who you hope to be when you are 85 (or 105, if age 85 is not far off for you). Show your drawings to each other. (Two or three people may explain what they drew, if time allows.)

SESSION 2 VIDEO (10 minutes)

Watch and discuss the video for session two.

TO DO (5 minutes)

Review the steps each participant should take before the next session:

→ **Read** chapter two of *Free*.

→ **Work through** the steps to creating a time budget described in the chapter.

→ **Choose** one of the following activities to try and report your experience to the group the next time you meet:

→ **Spend** 5-20 minutes a day sitting in stillness to confront hurry.

→ **Plan and take** a 24-hour restorative Sabbath.

→ **Fast** from media for one week.

CLOSE (5 minutes)

Have someone in the group read Psalm 139:1-6, 13-16 aloud.

Optional Daily Readings Before the Next Session

→ The Creator's presence in this moment (Psalm 139)

→ The way Jesus saw time and opportunity (John 7:1-9)

→ Jesus unhurried in pursuit of his goals (Luke 13:21-35)

→ Jesus on the purpose of the Sabbath (Mark 2:23-27)

→ Make the most of your time (Ephesians 5:8-20)

→ Mary and Martha: "Only one thing is needed" (Luke 10:38-42)

→ Jesus teaches on watchfulness (Luke 12:35-48)

SESSION 3

Value and Align Your Time

Goals for this session:

→ Reflect on feelings about time.

→ Explore what the group learned through doing time-related experiments (sabbath keeping, daily stillness, media fast).

→ Process what came up for group members while creating their time budgets.

→ Investigate the trade-offs we often make between time, money and meaning and the possibility of taking new risks to pursue what matters most.

PRAYER (5 minutes)

Read "A Prayer of Abundance (for group use)" on page 227 aloud together.

CHAPTER DISCUSSION (10 minutes)

What thoughts, insights or questions came up for you as you worked through the exercises in chapter two?

Which of the feelings and messages about time do you most relate to (see pp. 67-68)? Explain.

What disciplines for managing and prioritizing time have worked for you? What is one new step you would like to take to spend your time pursuing what matters most?

SCRIPTURE (10 minutes)

The way Jesus responded when his brothers pushed him to make a public appearance reveals something significant about his understanding of time. Have someone from the group read John 7:1-9 aloud, then reflect as a group on how this passage speaks to the invitation to live without hurry and from a deeper sense of purpose and presence.

What does this passage reveal about how Jesus saw his time and work?

How did Jesus' sense of time differ from the assumptions of his brothers?

Describe a time you experienced a sense that it was "the right time"—that you were exactly where you should be.

HUDDLE (35 minutes)

Divide into groups of three or four (preferably the same people from the last session) and check in on the experiment you chose and the task of the week.

Discuss your experience of "Being Watchful and Present" (p. 69). Do you find it easy or difficult to be still? Explain.

What helps you be aware of God's presence?

If you decided to practice stillness as a daily experiment, what did you notice and discover as a result?

If you did the media fast as your experiment, how was your experience? What did abstaining from media reveal for you?

How would you like to integrate what you learned into the ongoing rhythm of your life?

If you decided to experiment with sabbath-keeping, how was your experience? What did the commitment to rest for a full twenty-four hours reveal?

Is this a practice that you hope to continue? What would you need to do to make that possible?

Take five minutes for each person to share about creating a time budget, using the following questions as a guide.

→ What stood out to you? Were there any surprises in where your time is going?

→ Which activities do you want to spend more time on as a reflection of your deeper values and goals?

→ What do you think you'll have to say no to in order to align your time with what matters most?

→ What are the trade-offs you are making between money and time? Do you need to give up some time to earn more money, or would you like to earn less to spend more time doing what matters most to you? Are you happy with the tradeoffs, or would you like to make different choices? Why?

→ What do you hear the Spirit nudging you toward in regard to how you spend your time?

RISK BEING FULLY ALIVE (10 minutes)

Reunite as a larger group. Chapter two concludes with a series of questions. Sometimes healthy change comes gradually, and at other times a more radical shift is necessary. Either way it can be helpful to dream about and consider what taking a big risk might look like.

Write each of the questions below on a separate piece of large paper.

→ What longing to do good have you been putting on hold?

→ What does your heart long to be and do? What would you choose to do today if you let your deeper passions lead you?

→ What is the craziest thing you can imagine doing that would free up your time and your life to do what you are most passionate about?

SESSION 3 VIDEO (10 minutes)

Watch and discuss the video for session two.

TO DO (5 minutes)

Review the steps each participant should take before the next session:

- → **Read** chapter three of *Free*.
- → **Complete** the assets of abundance survey on pages 95-96.
- → **Choose** two experiments to try from the suggestions below:
- → **Celebrate** your abundance (p. 98).
- → **Keep** a daily gratitude log for seven days (p. 98). Bring your gratitude log to the next session to share.
- → **Work** through steps to confronting worry (p. 100).
- → **Try** the "Ask. Seek. Knock." challenge (p. 108).

CLOSE (5 minutes)

Have someone read Ecclesiastes 3:1-8, or sit in silence.

Optional Daily Readings Before the Next Session

- → The Maker's provision for all living things (Psalm 145)
- → Giving thanks for the enduring love of God (Psalm 118; 136)
- → Ask. Seek. Knock. (Matthew 7:7-11)
- → Miraculous provision for a crowd (Matthew 14:15-21)
- → Parable of the persistent widow (Luke 18:1-8)
- → A life without worry and fear (Matthew 6:23-32)
- → A mind and heart transformed by trust (Philippians 4:4-9)

SESSION 4

Practice Gratitude and Trust

Goals for this session:

- → Support one another in taking steps of gratitude and trust.
- → Reflect on the role that fear and worry have played in our lives.
- → Consider whether we can trust that what we need will be provided.

+ Recognize the benefits and importance of gratitude.
+ Cultivate practices of gratitude and trust.

PRAYER (5 minutes)

Have two or three people share excerpts from their gratitude log poems as a prayer of thanks.

CHAPTER DISCUSSION (15 minutes)

What thoughts, insights or questions came up for you as you worked through the concepts and exercises in chapter three?

As a group process the exercise "Appreciate Your Assets of Abundance" (pp. 95-96).

+ In terms of our global context, how well are your needs being met?
+ Are you generally satisfied with what you have? Why or why not?
+ Which nonmonetary/nonmaterial assets do you enjoy and appreciate the most?
+ Why do you think we tend to overvalue material possessions and undervalue other assets of abundance?

HUDDLE (20 minutes)

Divide into smaller groups and check in on the recommended experiments for the week.

If you chose to do the experiment "Celebrate Your Abundance," what did you learn about practicing gratitude through celebration and feasting?

If you chose to keep a daily gratitude log, what did you discover? How did this practice shape you this week?

Did you attempt the experiment of asking God for what you need over the next thirty days? If so, what's on your list?

SCRIPTURE: WHY DO YOU WORRY? (30 minutes)

Reunite as a larger group. Have each group member write down their worries on a pad of sticky notes, one worry for each sticky notes. Stick the notes on a wall as you go. After five minutes, stop writing and look over the wall of collected worries.

When you look at the wall of worries, what themes or patterns do you notice?

Why do you think we are prone to worry?

Take turns reading Matthew 6:25-34 three times.

+ After the first reading, share a word or phrase that spoke to you.

+ During the second reading, pay attention to the voice of Jesus in this passage. Share one word each that describes how Jesus' voice makes you feel.

+ After the third reading, discuss the questions below.

Do you believe you can trust the Creator to provide what you need? What in your experiences creates doubts about this? What in your experience confirms that what you need will be provided?

We are cared for, and we have enough. Yet millions of people are starving and struggle for basic health and safety. Can someone in such a desperate situation experience abundance? Does God provide enough for everyone?

Share a story or experience of having a need provided for in some miraculous or unusual way.

SESSION 4 VIDEO (10 minutes)

Watch and discuss the video for session four.

TO DO (5 minutes)

Review the steps each participant should take before the next session:

+ **Read** chapter four of *Free*.

+ **Practice** a discipline of contentment by voluntarily fasting for one week from something you normally enjoy.

+ **Consider adopting** a longer-term fast that you might share with a friend (see p. 121).

+ **Work through** the worksheet "Taking Steps Toward Voluntary Simplicity." Make a commitment to limit your consumption in key spending categories (p. 123).

+ **Begin** an experiment in decluttering and radical generosity. How might the instruction "If you have two coats, share with the one who has none" apply to your drawers and closets? Take an inventory of all of the clothing and shoes you own. Bring the clothing and shoes you are willing to sell or give away to your next group session. As a group, decide what to do with the collected clothes and whether to continue this experiment with books, electronics, collectibles and larger household items.

CLOSE (5 minutes)

Have two or three people share excerpts from their gratitude log poems aloud.

Optional Daily Readings Before the Next Session

+ Psalms of contentment (Psalm 131:1-2; Psalm 23)
+ The meaninglessness of striving (Ecclesiastes 5:10-15)
+ Enjoying what you have (Ecclesiastes 6:3-9)
+ Give and fast discretely (Matthew 6:1, 16-18)
+ A story about the folly of hoarding (Luke 12:13-21)
+ Jesus and the rich young ruler (Luke 18:18-29)
+ The wisdom of contentment (1 Timothy 6:6-9)

SESSION 5

Believe You Have Enough

Goals for this session:

+ Reflect on the ways we've been shaped by a sense of scarcity, greed and a hunger for more.
+ Explore how consumption relates to one's sense of satisfaction.
+ Support one another's steps toward voluntary limits.
+ Appreciate the connection between contentment and generosity.
+ Brainstorm and commit to a multiweek experiment in contentment and generosity ("Have Two, Give One").

PRAYER (5 minutes)

Read "A Prayer of Abundance (for group use)" on page 227 aloud together.

CHAPTER DISCUSSION (10 minutes)

What thoughts, insights or questions came up for you as you worked through the concepts and exercises in chapter four?

How do you relate to the struggle to believe you have enough and the temptation to think you need more to be happy?

Do voluntary limits seem more like a guilt-induced obligation or a kind invitation into a better way of life? Why?

What do you think are compelling reasons to place limits on consumption?

In which area (food and drink, clothing, housing, transportation, consumer goods, entertainment) would adopting voluntary limits be the most vital and have the most impact for you? Why?

What soul work do you think is required to experience true contentment and satisfaction?

HUDDLE (20 minutes)

Divide into smaller groups and check in on recommended experiments for the week.

What did you choose to fast from for seven days as an experiment in contentment? What did your fast reveal about your attachments?

In what areas did you choose to set a voluntary limit to consumption? How was your first week? Did you encounter any challenges or resistance to this commitment?

What do you think it's going to take for you to follow through with this change over time?

SCRIPTURE (10 minutes)

Reunite as a larger group. The parables and teachings of Jesus about the heart and material attachments challenge many of our popular notions about security and "the good life." Read Luke 12:13-21, 32-34 aloud. Reflect on how this passage speaks to the invitation to live a free, generous and trusting life.

Why do you think Jesus would tell his disciples, "Sell your possessions and give to the poor"? What did this instruction say about his understanding of how life works?

Is this instruction taken seriously by disciples of Jesus today? Why or why not? What would be different if it were?

HAVE TWO, GIVE ONE (25 minutes)

Sort through the clothes you've collected in the center of the room. Make two piles—one pile for the resale shop (if such a store exists in your area) and one pile for the thrift store. As you sort the piles, take any clothing items you need (remembering, of course, that you've all just decluttered your closets). Enlist someone from the group to take clothes to the resale shop and thrift shop. Make a plan for storing items if you decide to do a collective garage sale.

When you went through your closets and drawers this week, how did you decide what to keep and what to sell, share or give?

How do you want what you learned in this process to shape how you acquire clothes in the future?

Would this experiment be helpful and transformative to continue over the next three sessions? Why or why not?

If you do want to continue, start to chart out a plan. What will you collect each week (for example, smaller household items [books, music, hobbies, collectibles, etc.] for session six; larger household items [bicycles, televisions, appliances, sports equipment, vehicles, etc.] for session seven)? How will you sell, share or give these possessions? Set a date for a garage sale (before session eight) if that seems like a good option, and begin drafting a plan for the details—where items will be stored, how they'll be transported, who else in your community you might invite to participate. Begin to consider where to donate the proceeds (e.g., local or global organizations supporting the poor, or to pay down consumer debt for group members), and how to get rid of the "junk" that isn't in good enough shape to sell or donate. Designate group members to follow up on each of these tasks, then discuss the following questions.

What kind of resistance or questions come up for you as you contemplate continuing this activity?

What do you think are the proper motives for an experiment like this?

If "Have Two, Give One" seems too audacious for your group, what other experiment would you propose that would help you discover true security?

A practice like setting voluntary limits or giving away possessions works if you keep in mind why you are doing it and treat it as a playful exercise. Limiting or giving away possessions is a way to viscerally question assumptions about scarcity and greed. We can only know the freedom of abundance and voluntary limits by experience. So taking such a risk is a gift. Moreover, the experiment is voluntary; no one will be looking over your shoulder judging whether you've really gotten rid of half your shoes. Be playful about it; see how far you are comfortable going, and don't worry about anyone else.

SESSION 5 VIDEO (10 minutes)

Watch and discuss the video for session five.

TO DO (5 minutes)

Review the steps each participant should take before the next session.

+ **Read** chapter five of *Free*.

+ **Determine** the financial season you are currently in (see p. 147).

+ **Set** financial goals for the next one to three years in alignment with your deeper values and life goals using the worksheet on pages 151-53.

+ **Create** a realistic spending plan, including income projections and spending in fixed and flexible categories. Come to the next session prepared to share your spending plan with your group or huddle. *Group leaders should decide which option is best for the group.* Bring copies of your spending plan for each person in your group.

+ **Have two, give one.** If your group decided to continue this experiment, go through your small household items (books, DVDs, small electronics, collectibles, etc.). Sell selected items online, and bring sharable items to the next session for your group garage sale.

CLOSE (5 minutes)

Have someone read Psalm 131:1-2 aloud.

Optional Daily Readings Before the Next Session

+ Parallels between managing money and spiritual riches (Luke 16:10-13)

+ Counting the cost before you spend (Luke 14:25-33)

+ A community of trust and interdependence (Acts 2:42-47)

+ Should we pay taxes? (Matthew 17:24-27)

+ The unique way Jesus paid his taxes (Luke 20:20-25)

+ Promises about giving a tenth of income away (Malachi 3:6-12)

+ The value and importance of financial planning (Proverbs 21:5; 24:3-4)

SESSION 6

Create a Spending Plan

Goals for this session:

+ Reflect on the challenges and benefits of using a spending plan.

+ Explore the dynamics that help create a community of trust, support and interdependence.

+ Take the risk to share spending plans with one another.

+ Support each other to make wise financial management choices.

PRAYER (5 minutes)

Read "A Prayer of Abundance (for group use)" on page 227 aloud together.

HAVE TWO, GIVE ONE (5 minutes)

If your group elected to continue with this experiment, take a few minutes to check in and get organized.

Make a pile of the smaller household items and valuables you've collected in the middle of the room. Look through the items and take one or two items you need (remembering, of course, that you've all just decluttered your homes).

When you went through your small household items this week, how did you decide what to keep and what to sell, share or give away?

What thoughts or questions have come up for you as you have engaged in this process?

What tips or recommendations do you have about how to sell or where to donate or recycle items?

CHAPTER DISCUSSION (15 minutes)

What thoughts, insights or questions came up for you as you worked through the concepts and exercises in chapter five?

Can you relate to any of the reasons for resistance to using a spending plan described on pages 144-46? Explain.

What do you think are the benefits of creating and using a spending plan? How have you experienced those benefits personally?

How might a spending plan help a person use their time and money to pursue what matters most?

SCRIPTURE (15 minutes)

One of the most remarkable aspects of the early Jesus movement was how his life and teachings inspired people to care for one another's material needs. Read Acts 2:42-47 aloud and reflect on how this passage speaks to the possibility of mutual support, trust and interdependence.

What is attractive to you about this description of community?

What do you suppose allowed this group to be so open, trusting and generous with one another? Would that be possible today? Why or why not?

What are the cultural values and habits that inhibit us from being open, trusting and generous with one another?

How might sharing our spending plans be a first step toward a deeper level of community?

HUDDLE (15 minutes)

Divide into smaller groups and check in on recommended tasks and exercises for the week.

What financial season are you currently in? What are the main financial priorities that are appropriate for you in this season?

What are your short-term financial goals—spending and giving, debt reduction, work and earning, saving and investing?

Do your next steps seem realistic and doable, or do you have some anxiety or concern about achieving these goals? Explain.

SHARE YOUR SPENDING PLANS (25 minutes)

You can do this activity by continuing in smaller huddle groups or reunite as a larger group. Sharing spending plans in huddle groups may feel less intimidating; doing so as a larger group can bond the whole group but will take more time. You could also opt to have half the group share in this session and the other half in session seven. Before you begin, refer to tips on page 161.

What excites you or scares you about sharing your spending plan?

Take turns sharing your spending plans with one another, passing out a paper copy to each person. Allow each person seven to ten minutes to share their process.

As you worked through the steps to creating a spending plan, what stood out to you? What surprised you? Where did you feel the most challenged or encouraged?

What feelings came up for you during this process?

What questions came up that you are still trying to answer?

Where in your financial goals and spending plan do you recognize a particular opportunity to trust God?

Which aspect of your financial goals and spending plan will require the most intentional effort or discipline to achieve?

Reflect on the following questions after each person has shared.

+ What stood out to you about this person's spending plan?

+ Is there a clarifying question you would like to ask? What helpful words of advice or encouragement do you have for the person who has just shared?

+ How can the group support this person in achieving their goals? How can the group pray for this person right now?

SESSION 6 VIDEO (10 minutes)

Watch and discuss the video for session six.

TO DO (5 minutes)

Review the steps each participant should take before the next session.

+ **Read** chapter six of *Free*.

+ **Take** any further steps necessary to enacting your spending plan. Organize your financial files and record keeping. If you haven't already, set up a method for how you will handle cash and pay expenses in each category of your spending plan (cash, check, auto payment, credit card). Set up a method to track your monthly earning and spending using a spreadsheet or personal finance application.

+ If you currently have debts, **work through** a plan for reducing or eliminating debt.

→ Try at least one new economizing practice.

→ **Have two, give one.** If your group decided to continue this experiment, go through your larger household items (bicycles, furniture, appliances, automobiles, etc.). Sell some items and bring sharable items to the next session for your group garage sale.

CLOSE (2 minutes)

Recite the Lord's prayer together (Matthew 6:9-13).

Optional Daily Readings Before the Next Session

→ Warnings and advice about lending and borrowing (Proverbs 6:1-11)

→ A story about being shrewd and resourceful (Luke 16:1-9)

→ Paul's perspective on work, earning and giving (Acts 20:32-35)

→ Wise sayings about wealth, debt and work (Proverbs 22:1-16, 26-27)

→ Let love be your only outstanding debt (Romans 13:8)

→ On saving and gathering wealth slowly (Proverbs 13:11; 28:18-20)

→ Resourcefulness and frugality in the feeding of many (Matthew 14:13-21)

SESSION 7

Maximize Your Resources

Goals for this session:

→ Reflect on the connection between the management of material resources and spiritual riches and enlightenment.

→ Explore how the prevalence of debt affects our economy and personal lives.

→ Share best practices for maximizing resources.

→ Support one another in taking steps to maximize resources.

PRAYER (5 minutes)

Read "A Prayer of Abundance (for group use)" on page 227 aloud together.

HAVE TWO, GIVE ONE (5 minutes)

If your group elected to continue with this experiment, take a few minutes to check in and get organized.

Did you decide to divest of any larger household items this past week? What did you sell? Where did you find success selling items?

> → Finalize where you would like to donate the proceeds from the possessions you've sold or plan to sell, based on whatever research group members have done. Remember that it may be wise for some people in your group to use proceeds from the sale of their possessions to pay down consumer debts. Money will be pooled at the next session.

SHARE YOUR SPENDING PLANS (20 minutes)

Share whatever group members' spending plans weren't shared at the previous session. Refer to the guiding questions for this activity in session six. For the sake of time you may omit sharing hot tips for economizing (see below).

CHAPTER DISCUSSION (10 minutes)

What thoughts, insights or questions came up for you as you worked through the concepts and exercises in chapter six?

Do frugality and resourcefulness have positive or negative associations for you? Explain.

SCRIPTURE (15 minutes)

Jesus made some surprising connections between the management of material resources and the true riches of God's kingdom. Read Luke 16:1-15 aloud and reflect on how this passage speaks to the stewardship of resources. This is one of the more complex and perplexing passages in the Gospels; it both praises shrewd resourcefulness and warns against "the love of money." You may want to consult a Bible commentary to frame your conversation.

In the story, the master commends the manager for acting shrewdly to collect debts. How might this have been different from the way he had previously managed the master's possessions?

Luke 16:9 is one of the more curious sayings attributed to Jesus. What do you think he meant by "use worldly wealth to gain friends"?

What do you suppose it means to be "trustworthy" with your possessions?

What might be the difference between being shrewd and being stingy?

Where have you seen an example of someone who has been trustworthy with little become entrusted with much?

HUDDLE (20 minutes)

Divide into smaller groups and check in on recommended tasks and exercises for the week.

What is your method for handling cash and paying for expenses in each category of your spending plan?

How are you tracking your monthly earning and spending (using a spreadsheet or personal finance application)?

How orderly and easily accessible are your financial records and files?

What steps have you taken to avoid debt or pay down debts that you feel good about?

Are you comfortable with the amount of money you owe to others? What are your current total loan obligations?

Does the amount you currently owe affect your sense of well-being or your freedom to pursue what matters most? Explain.

What new choices would you like to make to help you pay down your debts or avoid debt in the future? What is your debt-reduction plan?

HOT TIPS ON ECONOMIZING (25 minutes)

Reunite as a larger group. On a large sheet of paper, make a list of common spending categories that are relevant to your group (housing, utilities, food, transportation, healthcare, clothing, entertainment/travel, debt reduction, education, etc.). Pass around a $20 bill as a "talking stick" as group members share an economizing strategy that has worked for them in various areas.

On a separate sheet of paper, list the main economizing strategies from chapter six (pp. 174-82). Using the "talking stick" again, share tips and best practices.

At the end of this brainstorming session, have each person share one or two economizing practices they are committed to renewing or trying for the first time.

SESSION 7 VIDEO (10 minutes)

Watch and discuss the video for session six.

TO DO (5 minutes)

Review the steps each participant should take before the next session.

→ **Read** chapter seven and the conclusion to *Free*.

→ **Estimate** your relative wealth in comparison with global standards. Visit globalrichlist.com and enter your total yearly income to calculate your global wealth ranking.

→ **Determine** next-step practices in the following four categories, using the worksheet at the end of chapter seven:

  → Be a friend to the poor

  → Spend consciously

  → Choose meaningful work and service

  → Invest wisely

→ **Execute** your collective garage sale (if you choose this option as a group). Let shoppers know which organization, if any, that proceeds are going toward. Share or thrift any items that don't sell.

→ If you haven't made a final decision, **investigate** which organizations and causes your group might like to give the money you've collected.

→ **Bring** the proceeds from items you sold to the final session to be contributed to the organization(s) you chose as a group.

→ **Prepare** a delicious meal or dessert item to share at the final session.

CLOSE (5 minutes)

Have someone in the group read Psalm 23 aloud.

Optional Daily Readings Before the Next Session

  → An invitation to true fasting (Isaiah 58:1-12)

  → "Whatever you do for the least of these" (Matthew 25:31-46)

  → A story about risk and investment (Matthew 25:14-30)

  → Wise sayings about work and money (Proverbs 11)

  → Instructions on giving discretely (Matthew 6:1-4)

  → A pattern for collecting and distributing funds (2 Corinthians 8–9)

  → On showing favoritism based on wealth (James 2:1-12)

SESSION 8

Live Generously and Spend Wisely

Goals for this session:

+ Appreciate that we vote with our spending.

+ Consider where you want to give your time, talents and financial resources.

+ Recognize the costs and benefits to adopting a more ethical, globally conscious and local lifestyle and spending practices.

+ Imagine the ways we can create a culture of abundance and a sharing economy.

+ Discuss ethical purchasing and investment practices.

SIMPLICITY SELF-ASSESSMENT AND FUND COLLECTION (10 minutes)

Turn in any money you wish to contribute to group giving. Fill out the simplicity self-assessment (see below).

PRAYER (5 minutes)

Read "A Prayer of Abundance (for group use)" on page 227 aloud together.

CHAPTER DISCUSSION (5 minutes)

What thoughts, insights or questions came up for you as you worked through the concepts and exercises in chapter seven?

GROUP EXERCISE: HOW WEALTHY ARE YOU? (10 minutes)

Note: You will need enough pennies for each person to have one penny for every thousand dollars they make a year. If you aren't prepared with pennies on hand, skip the exercise and move directly to the discussion questions.

Make a pile of five pennies for each person, to represent the amount in thousands ($5,000) that the average person in the world earns each year. Then make a second pile of pennies representing the annual income of your household (one penny per $1000). Share your global wealth ranking (from globalrichlist.com) with the group. Then collect all the pennies from the first piles (5 pennies x number of group members) into one group, and the remaining pennies into another pile, representing the group's collective wealth.

Did the results of this exercise surprise you? Explain.

Given your level of wealth relative to the rest of the world, do you have enough? Why do you think we are more likely to compare ourselves with people who are more well off than we are than with those who are less well off than we are?

What does our relative privilege in terms of monetary wealth suggest about the opportunity to live generously and spend wisely?

SCRIPTURE (15 minutes)

In the story of the sheep and the goats (Matthew 25:31-46) Jesus echoes the ancient call to care for the hungry, thirsty, naked, sick and lonely. Read Isaiah 58:1-12 aloud, and reflect on how this passage speaks to the invitation to live generously and spend wisely.

Why was the prophet sent to correct the nation of Israel? In what ways do we today tend to miss the connection between seeking God and caring for the least of these?

Who are the orphans and widows, the hungry and naked, the exploited and oppressed in our world today? In our local community?

How does your heart long to act on behalf of those who suffer?

What is the promise in this passage for those who seek to care for the hungry, thirsty, naked, lonely and oppressed?

Who is most in need of healing—those with resources or those without? Explain.

HUDDLE (15 minutes)

Divide into smaller groups and check in on recommended tasks and exercises for the chapter.

What next steps did you identify for yourself in each of these categories?

+ Being a friend to the poor
+ Spending more consciously (or voting with your spending) as funds become available
+ Choosing meaningful work and service
+ Investing wisely

EVALUATE YOUR EXPERIENCE (20 minutes)

Reunite as a larger group and reflect on your experience together for the past eight sessions.

What was the most influential aspect of participating in this group learning experience?

What tasks, exercises or experiments were most helpful to you?

What step have you taken in this process that you are most proud of?

As you worked through the steps in this book, where have you encountered the most resistance within yourself?

What might this resistance reveal about a deeper level of disordered attachment? How have you felt the whisper of the Spirit inviting you into fuller freedom?

What kind of ongoing support might help you continue the journey to becoming free to spend your time and money on what matters most?

What are some practical ideas for what this group might do to stay connected and continue to support each other to spend time and money on what matters most?

APPRECIATIONS (5 minutes)

Take turns sharing what you have most appreciated about going through this process together.

CLOSE (5 minutes)

Read the poem at the end of the book's conclusion aloud as a benediction to your time together as a group.

Self-Evaluation

What was the most influential aspect of participating in this group learning experience?

What tasks, exercises or experiments were most helpful to you?

What step have you taken in this process that you are most proud of?

What advice or encouragement would you give to someone considering taking these steps? What do you wish you would have known before starting this process?

Which steps in this process would you like to revisit and work on more?

* Name What Matters Most to You
* Value and Align Your Time
* Practice Gratitude and Trust
* Believe You Have Enough
* Create a Spending Plan
* Maximize Your Resources
* Live Generously and Spend Wisely

In which of the following areas have you experienced the most growth, change or new clarity during this process?

Work & Meaning	Soul Issues	Global Sustainability
Time Management	Money Management	

As you worked through the steps in this book, where have you encountered the most resistance within yourself?

What might this reveal about a deeper level of disordered attachment? How have you felt the whisper of the Spirit inviting you into fuller freedom?

What kind of ongoing support might help you continue the journey to becoming free to spend your time and money on what matters most?

What are some practical ideas for what this group might do to stay connected and continue to support each other to spend time and money on what matters most?

Would you recommend this process to a friend?

☐ Yes ☐ No ☐ Maybe

Is this a process you would be interesting in helping facilitate for others in the future?

☐ Yes ☐ No ☐ Maybe

What changes would make this group learning experience better?

Thanks for your honest reflections and valuable feedback!

Mark Scandrette is the founding director of Reimagine, a center for integral Christian practice based in San Francisco, where he leads an annual series of retreats, learning labs, conversations and projects designed to help participants integrate the teachings of Jesus into every aspect of life through shared practices and community experiments. A sought-after voice for creative, radical and embodied Christian practice, he speaks nationally and internationally at conferences, universities and churches, offering training and coaching to leaders and organizations. Mark is also the author of *Practicing the Way of Jesus* (InterVarsity Press, 2011) and *Soul Graffiti* (Jossey-Bass, 2007).

Lisa Scandrette makes a life in the Mission District of San Francisco with Mark, Hailey, Noah and Isaiah. She spends her time teaching kids, facilitating workshops and doing administrative work with ReIMAGINE, and creating with her hands. She specializes in living simply and offering care and hospitality.

For booking information and inquiries visit
www.markscandrette.com.

ReImagine is a center for integral Christian practice based in San Francisco. The mission of ReImagine is to help people experience greater wholeness through the life and teachings of Jesus and to empower leaders who can create communities of transformation. Our dream is to see leaders and communities of living practice cultivated and supported across the United States and around the world. We pursue this dream by communicating vision, creating resources, inviting participants into transformational group experiments and developing leaders who can guide others. For more information visit

www.reimagine.org

FREE VIDEO CHAT WITH THE AUTHORS

If you are working through *Free* with a group of people, the authors would love to interact with your group via a free twenty-minute video chat. Simply be one of the first fifty groups to make your request by contacting

Info@reimagine.org

POOL RESOURCES ONLINE

Now that you've completed the journey through Free, take the next step and join Common Change, a free online tool that allows you to pool resources with others in your group and be generous by meeting the needs of others in your lives. Learn more, contact us, or sign up today at CommonChange.com!

COMMON CHANGE

LIKEWISE. *Go and do.*

A man comes across an ancient enemy, beaten and left for dead. He lifts the wounded man onto the back of a donkey and takes him to an inn to tend to the man's recovery. Jesus tells this story and instructs those who are listening to "go and do likewise."

Likewise books explore a compassionate, active faith lived out in real time. When we're skeptical about the status quo, Likewise books challenge us to create culture responsibly. When we're confused about who we are and what we're supposed to be doing, Likewise books help us listen for God's voice. When we're discouraged by the troubled world we've inherited, Likewise books encourage us to hold onto hope.

In this life we will face challenges that demand our response. Likewise books face those challenges with us so we can act on faith.

ivpress.com/likewise
twitter.com/likewise_books
facebook.com/likewisebooks
youtube.com/likewisebooks